LIVE YOUR DREAM – PART ONE

A Canadian Couple's Exploration of USA Highways
and Byways by Motorcycle

by
Roney Cubbon and Colin Nielsen

Order this book online at www.trafford.com
or email orders@trafford.com

Most Trafford titles are also available at major online book retailers.

Note for Librarians: A cataloguing record for this book is available from Library
and Archives Canada at www.collectionscanada.ca/amicus/index-e.html

Printed in Victoria, BC, Canada.

ISBN: 978-1-4269-1100-2

*Our mission is to efficiently provide the world's finest, most comprehensive book publishing
service, enabling every author to experience success. To find out how to publish your
book, your way, and have it available worldwide, visit us online at www.trafford.com*

Trafford rev. 10/02/2009

 www.trafford.com

North America & international
toll-free: 1 888 232 4444 (USA & Canada)
phone: 250 383 6864 ♦ fax: 812 355 4082

ACKNOWLEDGEMENTS:

We are grateful to the many people who helped and encouraged us to fulfill our dream of writing this, our first motorcycle adventure book.

First of all, we would like to thank Sean and Ian Layfield and Gary Lee, who made it possible for us to leave Victoria for four months by looking after Roney's home during our absence. Without them this trip would not have been possible.

Our heartfelt thanks go out to the many people we met along the way; at gas stations, B & B's, Inns, Hotels, monuments, parks, and at motorcycle shops, who encouraged us to write about our trip. To the many wonderful hosts it was our privilege to meet, thank you for your hospitality. A special thanks to Phil Boucher at the Motorcycle Accessory Centre in Calgary for always being available to us throughout the trip, you are a man with amazing contacts and really care about your customers. To the many helpful people we met in the various motorcycle service shops that serviced our bikes along the way, an especially big thank you for your great customer service. We also very much appreciated access to computers and the internet from the many Public Libraries that we visiting throughout our trip. This trip proved to us that there is such an amazing bond between those of us who ride. A very special thank you to a good friend, Mickey Huston, for her encouragement, proofing and suggestions for writing this book.

LIVE YOUR DREAM

–

PART ONE

Introduction:

The idea of a long motorcycle trip through the United States first came about when Roney and I discovered our shared passion for motorcycle riding on the open road. We met in January 2005 and later that spring and summer took three rides together which got us thinking about a much longer ride around the United States. The idea of doing the traditional **Four Corners** at breakneck speed, without stopping to 'smell the roses', didn't appeal to us. We decided that a more enjoyable way to explore the USA would be to take our time, spend as much time as possible riding Federal, State and County routes and avoiding, as much as possible, the Interstate Freeway Network.

It took us two years of planning to see everything put into motion and to realize that this, our "dream" ride of a lifetime, was really possible. We started serious planning for our trip during the winter of 2006/07. We had a couple of real pluses going for us: (1) we were both retired thus had the time to take a long trip and (2) we had a number of time-share weeks that we were able to trade for 6 weeks of timeshare accommodations at strategic places around the USA, providing us with places to rest, do laundry, explore locally and get our bikes serviced. We were successful in booking a week in Upstate New York, in Williamsburg, Virginia, in Ft Lauderdale, FL, in New Orleans, in Branson, MO and in Las Vegas. We gave ourselves two weeks between each of these timeshare weeks for travel and exploration which we were to discover was not quite enough time.

Part of our pre-trip planning was spent surfing the Internet for information on things to see and do and requesting Visitor Information packages from every state we planned to visit. Going through all of this information, after it was received, and picking those things that we definitely wanted to see was fun but time consuming. Even more important was getting our bikes equipped for such an extended trip. This included adding hard bags and trunks, round motorcycle suitcases as well as aftermarket pipes (we wanted to make sure we could be heard if not seen by other motorists). A trip to the Abbotsford, BC Motorcycle Show in February 2007 helped us find a few more "essential" items for the trip and, most importantly, a contact person in Calgary, Phil Boucher, at the Motorcycle Accessory Centre, who came in very handy during our trip.

Everything finally came together for us during April, 2007, and after careful packing, sorting, repacking to ensure we were just taking the basics in clothing and supplies and a final servicing of the bikes, we departed on our dream ride on April 29, 2007. We were about to have the education and pleasure of a trip most other bikers only dream about.

For those of you who have thought about a long trip by motorcycle, go out there and do it. The experience of meeting so many friendly and helpful people, both riders and non riders, expanded our horizons immensely. This trip also confirmed our perspective on the American people. They are just like us; friendly, helpful and very approachable. The wonders of America and the open road await you, so what's holding you back? If you do go, and you are Canadian, I hope you are as lucky as we were. The Canadian Dollar was near par, and at times, above the US dollar during our trip. This was another very fortunate occurrence for us.

We are Civil War buffs so this book is part American history, part travelogue, part open road adventure but most importantly, it is about the freedom that only motorcyclists can experience on the open road. Reliving our adventure through writing this book has been an experience almost equal to the ride itself. Our travels took us from Victoria British Columbia to New York; Huntsville, Alabama to Eureka, California; Manhattan, to San Diego; Leavenworth, Washington to Vacherie, Louisiana; Cody, WY to Key West, FL; in all we visited 35 States. By the time we returned home, we had ridden over 29,000 kilometers (about 18,000 miles). Many people along the way asked us what our favorite place or state was and, as the ride progressed, the answer became more difficult. Each state had its own attributes and the variety made the ride the trip of a lifetime.

We hope you enjoy this account of our US of A motorcycle adventure, one that we shall never forget and which we are very happy to be able to share with you. It is our challenge to you to take up the open road and go for a long ride with your best friend, or life partner just like we did! If motorcycle trips are not your thing, take up your personal dream and follow it, you won't regret it!

Roney Cubbon and Colin Nielsen
April 2009

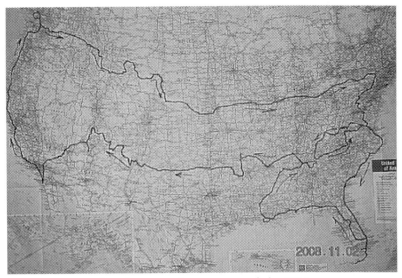
Our four month route around the USA.

INDEX

1.	Crossing the Northwestern USA	1
2.	Wyoming to New York	16
3.	New York	26
4.	Gettysburg, Washington & Williamsburg	43
5.	Williamsburg to Charlottesville	59
6.	West Virginia, Kentucky, Tennessee & North Carolina	67
7.	Virginia, Cape Hatteras to St. Augustine, FL	82
8.	St. Augustine to Del Ray Beach, FL..	92
9.	Del Ray Beach, the Bahamas & Orlando	104
10.	Orlando to New Orleans	111
11.	New Orleans to Tupelo, MS	118
12.	Tupelo, MS to Branson, MO	134
13.	Branson, MO to Oklahoma City	150
14.	Oklahoma City to Springdale, UT	157
15.	Springdale, UT to San Diego	171
16.	San Diego to Fort Bragg, CA	178
17.	Fort Bragg to Victoria – THE RIDE HOME	184
Epilogue		189
Lessons Learned		191
References		195

CHAPTER ONE – CROSSING THE NORTHWESTERN USA

After many hours of preparation, research, obtaining supplies and bike preparation, we left Victoria with a sense of anxiety, high expectations and a little apprehension, on the evening of April 29th, 2007, for the greatest adventure of our lives; a four month exploration of our Southern Neighbor, the United States of America.

Our rides were a new 2007 Kawasaki Vulcan 900 cc cruiser and a 2004 Honda VTX 1300 cc cruiser. We had worked hard to make the bikes as "bullet proof" as possible, adding many necessities as well as some 'nice to have' accessories. (See Lessons Learned for details). We'd spent many hours on the Internet researching sites to visit and had ordered Tourist Information Packages from every state we intended to visit. We'd culled this information down to one binder from boxes of information that we had received. We thought we had a pretty good basic route plan to follow. We had also traded six timeshare weeks for condo timeshare weeks in Upstate New York, Virginia, Florida, Louisiana, Missouri and Nevada. Our plans were to use each of these timeshare weeks as bases to explore those areas as well as to unwind, rest, do laundry and get our bikes serviced. (Good plan to have but we found we could have used more than one week to accomplish all that).

We started our trip from our home of Victoria, located on Vancouver Island off the Coast of British Columbia. We crossed Georgia Strait from Vancouver Island to the Mainland on our British Columbia Ferry system and spent the night with friends in Surrey, a suburb of Vancouver.

We left Surrey on April 30th, under partly cloudy skies and, after an hour wait at the border, we headed south on Interstate 5 to Everett, where we turned east onto US Highway 2. The excitement of this, our first day of many on the road, was impossible to contain. For those of you who ride, you know what we mean. Unlike driving a car, riding requires that the rider use all of their senses. The feel of the wind on your face, the aromas from freshly plowed fields and forests, the sound of the wind and bike, the sights both on and off the road, even the taste of the air, all are involved in riding. Riding gives one a feeling of freedom unequaled by anything else. We were exhilarated by the anticipation of four months of endless, challenging roads, new vistas and adventures around every corner. The reality of what we were doing really came to the fore when we exited Interstate 5 and headed east on Highway 2, a beautiful twisting highway through stunning mountain scenery over Stevens Pass in the Cascade Range.

We crossed over Stevens Pass where the summit (alt. 4061') still had 6' of compacted snow on the roadsides and it was cold! That night we stayed in Leavenworth, WA, a beautiful little Bavarian style Town in the Cascade Mountains of Northern Washington. As this was the first real night away from home on our long journey, we decided to splurge and stayed at a wonderful B&B called Anna's Haus Pension, which was designed like a Bavarian Chalet. Our room was very large and had a wonderful Jacuzzi tub in it, which we used to take out the stiffness of our first day's ride. If you haven't been to Leavenworth, it is a "must", you'll love it! It has the appearance of a town in the German or Swiss Alps. There is a large selection of boutique type shops, a great selection of restaurants and many tourist events are hosted throughout the year, making reservations advisable.

On the morning of May 1st, after a big European breakfast, we left Leavenworth and headed out on Highway 2, passing through

Wenatchee on our way east. It was a cold and cloudy day with intermittent rain. Our foul weather gear and heated vests were really essential, however our hands went **beyond** cold. Even with heated grips and good winter gloves, Roney's hands were unbearably cold. East of Wenatchee, Highway 2 rises up onto a high plateau, where it was even windier and colder. A couple of hours later we stopped in Coulee City for fuel and lunch. Seeing how cold we looked, our waitress asked us where we were heading, to which we replied all around the USA. Like so many others that we met along the way during our big ride, she was amazed. After returning to Highway 2, we continued our long and cold ride until we merged with Interstate 90 just west of Spokane, just in time for rush hour (WE have such a wonderful sense of timing)! We continued onto Coeur D'Alene, Idaho, where we stayed overnight in a converted Schoolhouse B&B called the Roosevelt Inn. Coeur D'Alene, for those of you who haven't been there, is a beautiful little city that is situated beside a stunning lake of the same name. It has one of the most beautiful settings in the Pacific Northwest, a combination of mountains, trees, gardens and water that is breath taking. After taking showers to "thaw out", we walked to a quaint little restaurant for dinner then discovered a hot tub in the garden area of our B & B where we decided to relax, thaw out and visit with other guests before turning in.

On May 2nd, after an awesome homemade breakfast and coffee, we left Coeur d'Alene under cloudy skies and rain, heading eastbound on I-90 to Missoula, Montana. So far, we had not seen the sun since leaving home, rain had been our constant companion. It rained nonstop all day. By now we were wondering whether the rain would ever stop (and we still had more weather surprises to come). We were not able to enjoy the mountainous terrain between Coeur d'Alene due to limited visibility, but we "knew" that better weather was bound to come! Late in the afternoon, we arrived in Missoula and booked into another nice B&B called the Goldsmith B & B, right beside the Blackfoot River. By the time we arrived, we were cold, fed up with the rain and thought that we might as well be **in** the river. Fortunately, our outer rain gear kept us dry and the heated vests kept our torsos warm. Our hard bags, round motorcycle suitcase and trunks repelled the all day rain and everything, except our exposed skin, stayed dry. By now, we were beginning to wonder if we had left too early in the year or whether we should have gone south down the West Coast first, but we'd booked our Condo time share weeks assuming we would go clockwise around the States, so we were committed to the Northern route. We were soon to realize that we had made the right choice.

On May 3rd, after a hardy breakfast, we headed east out of Missoula on Interstate 90. About an hour out it started to SNOW! The snow storm came upon us in seconds and soon snow was swirling all around us. We couldn't tell which direction it was coming from or going to. The wind started to blow in gusts making visibility a real challenge. The road was divided so we didn't have to worry about oncoming traffic, only vehicles approaching from behind. Colin wanted to wimp out and turn back, but Roney, brave soul that she is, said "NO - KEEP GOING – DON'T BE A WIMP", which hurt his manhood so he just had to go on. As we rode further east, the snowfall turned into a full blown blizzard. Here we were, two riders in an almost total whiteout riding down Interstate 90 at less than 10 mph, trying to see the yellow line on the right hand side of the right lane so we could stay on the road; at the same time we had to keep an eye on our rearview mirrors for overtaking semis or cars. Does the word crazy come to mind? Every few minutes, we had to clear our helmet visors, which fogged up inside and got covered with sticky snow on the outside. There are no wipers on motorcycle helmets! (Hmmmm, maybe that's something we should invent). We tried flipping our visors up but then the snow would get in our eyes. We also tried putting on our glasses with the visors up, and then our glasses steamed up and became covered with the sticky snow. We had no choice but to keep going, with Roney, turning back wasn't an option. Besides that, turning around in a virtual whiteout on an Interstate was unthinkable. After riding for some time, we came upon a truck stop and headed inside to warm up and wait for the storm to pass. We learned from the locals that the day before had been very hot, in fact the cashier said she wore shorts and a t-shirt to work that day. After an hour or so, the storm did let up and we continued east in more favorable conditions. Once we cleared the pass, we headed down to a beautiful valley where it was dry and sunny. There was no snow or any indication that it had snowed for some time. We had lunch, fueled up and felt much better. There was a field of horses nearby kicking up dust, running free and wild. The smell of dry hay in the air and a warm sweet smell of spring flowers made us quickly forget the blizzard. Life is good. This was living in the present at its best.

Never was anyone so happy to see Butte, Montana as we were. We checked into the first B& B that we saw, which just happened to be a million dollar B&B (NO KIDDING)! Toad Hall Manor B&B consisted of 11,000 incredible square feet with every amenity you could imagine, including an elevator. It was located on an 18 hole golf course in a very upscale area. "Mr. Toad" (Glenn) and his wife (Jane) were our wonderful hosts. Mr. Toad even gave us a ride uptown that evening for dinner in his beautiful stock 1956 THUNDERBIRD! He phoned for a reservation for us and, not only that, he picked us up afterward. Boy, talk about service. If you ever find yourself in Butte, we highly recommend the Uptown Cafe. The food is marvelous and the prices are very reasonable. We enjoyed the Toad Hall Manor and Butte so much, we stayed for two days to explore the area and to enjoy the Montana hospitality. Mr. Toad told us lots about the area, its history and about "speakeasies", what they were and how they came to be. Briefly, speakeasies were concealed places, perhaps underneath a hotel, where men could go to meet and drink hard liquor during Prohibition. In those dark days, many women thought if there was no liquor served anywhere in public places then their men would stay at home but, alas, speakeasies were built in secret places and they became very popular. We were told that the men would just say they were going out to friends to visit for a while, yeah right!

On Saturday May 5, just as we were headed out of Butte, we came upon a gun show. Gun shows are almost unheard of in Canada, so we stopped in for a look. Here were two innocent Canucks looking at many tables full of automatic and semi automatic weapons, many of which we hadn't even seen on TV before. And all for sale. Talk about the Wild West, it was quite an insight for us. We enjoyed talking to the various vendors and looking at the amazing collection of guns and ammo.

We headed east out of Butte on I-90, this time without snow, sleet or rain; just cloudy. We turned south at Whitehall, Montana onto State Highway 55 to Highway 41, then east onto Highway 287. This took us through the authentic western towns of Nevada City and Virginia City, the latter even has an authentic boot hill cemetery. The rolling landscape in this part of Montana quickly reminds one why Montana is known as the "Big Sky" state. After a photo stop, we continued on to the city of West Yellowstone, where we stayed at the West Yellowstone B&B, located 4 miles west of the Park entrance. While we were checking in, a herd of Buffalo, consisting of cows, calves and yearlings, came by and grazed their way through our host's front yard. These animals look so big when you are standing on the ground near them. Our hostess said this was only the second time this had happened. It really looked quite funny. While Roney was taking some pictures she even shooed one out of the yard (brave girl that she is)!

Sunday, May 6th, we awoke to our first brilliant sunny day. The highlight of our morning breakfast was the best homemade cinnamon bread, made in a bread maker, served with hot chocolate. What a treat. Finally, the weather was turning nice and we started the day with renewed enthusiasm for the great adventure that lay ahead. We had absolutely perfect conditions to travel through Yellowstone Park. A very helpful Ranger at the Park entrance told us about the NPS Annual Pass, which would allow two motorcycle riders on separate bikes, to enter most National Parks and Monuments throughout the United States for one full year from the date of purchase. We bought the pass for $85.00, what a deal this turned out to be for us! We rode straight through to see Old Faithful, who erupted for our viewing pleasure right on time. After enjoying a nice lunch in the Lodge, we talked to some fellow bikers, after they saw our BC license plates and exchanged stories. Then we set out to tour some more of the park, seeing lots of buffalo, elk, deer and one very friendly chipmunk along the way. Before leaving the Park, we went over Sylvan Pass (alt. 8530') which had opened only a week before after being closed for the winter season. We left Yellowstone via the east entrance, which still had lots of compacted snow along its shoulders. After riding slowly on 10 miles of gravel, we had our best ride yet. The road and scenery between Yellowstone and Cody, Wyoming is downhill and curvy with spectacular scenery around every corner. Riding in that valley, beside a stream, we saws mountain goats on the mountainsides. I think we need to invent a camera that can be mounted on our helmets, as taking photos from a moving motorcycle makes as much sense as talking on a cell phone on a moving motorcycle!

At Cody, we checked into the Lambright B&B and were treated like family by our hosts, Jim and Mary Crow. Jim and Mary were wonderful hosts. Jim told us of many interesting things about Cody, including the fact that it was founded and laid out by Buffalo Bill Cody, the legendary frontiersman and creator of the "Wild West Show" that toured the eastern USA and Europe from 1880 through 1910. Cody has an incredible museum called (surprise) the Buffalo Bill Museum. It has four exhibit areas including the largest private American gun collection in the world, with over 2700 firearms. Jim is quite a history buff and told us about a local church that was built by Buffalo Bill after he lost a hand in a poker game; the bet was that whoever lost that hand had to build a new church. We also had a long discussion with him about Custer's Last Stand at the Little Big Horn, which Jim had been researching for some time. Jim drove us around town and he and Mary really made us feel right at home. He even loaned us his passes for the Museum. Jim also phoned ahead and made a reservation with the owner of the historic Occidental Hotel in Buffalo, Wyoming, where we would be staying the following night. Wyoming has wonderful beef and we had the best steak dinner during the entire trip in Cody that evening at the Wyoming Rib & Chop House.

The following day, Monday May 7th, we left Cody and headed north for Billings, Montana to visit the Little Big Horn National Monument. We rode up Highway 14 to Deaver, WY, then headed north on Highway 310 to Interstate 90, then east to the Crow Agency, in eastern Montana. The memorial to General Custer and his 7th Cavalry is very moving. For us, it was a surreal feeling to be in the exact location where General Custer (Yellow Hair) led his troops to their deaths. The location is on top of a small hill on the Crow Indian Reserve. It has an interpretive Centre run by descendents of the Natives who fought at the Battle of the Little Big Horn. There are markers for locations where the various cavalrymen lost their lives, including markers on the hill where Custer and 41 of his troopers were killed. We learned that many of General Custer's troops were immigrants, some had arrived in New York from starving Ireland and many were also veterans of the Civil War. There is also a marker some distance from the top of the hill where it is thought that several troops tried to get to the river and escape the carnage but met their demise instead. There is also a cenotaph for the horses of the 7th Cavalry that were killed during the battle.

For those of you who enjoy history as we do, we learned a lot about the Little Big Horn that we would like to share with you. The battle of the Little Big Horn took place on June 25 and 26, 1876 at a location now called the Crow Agency MT. The native tribes included Lakota, Northern Cheyenne and Arapaho Indians, lead by Crazy Horse, Sitting Bull and Chief Gall. They were attempting to escape the cavalry and lead their people away from reserve lands that the troops wanted to force them onto. They had between 900 and 1,800 warriors (approximately 949 lodges). The battle was the most famous action of the Great Sioux War of 1876-77, and was a remarkable victory for the Lakota and Northern Cheyenne, led by Sitting Bull. The U.S. Seventh Cavalry, including a column of 700 men led by George Armstrong Custer, was utterly defeated. Five of the Seventh's companies were annihilated; Custer himself was killed as were two of his brothers, a nephew, and a brother-in-law.

In the months after the battle, Sitting Bull and his people fled the United States to Wood Mountain, Saskatchewan, Canada. In Canada, three Mounties rode into his camp and explained the Queen's rules to him and told them they had nothing to fear from the American Cavalry as long as they behaved and did not disturb the Canadian Native tribes. The bravery of the Mounties so impressed Sitting Bull that he and his people lived a peaceful life until their return to the United States in 1881. Only a small remnant of his band under Chief Wambligi decided to stay at Wood Mountain, in Canada. After his return to the United States, Sitting Bull briefly toured as a performer in Buffalo Bill's Wild West show. After working as a performer, Sitting Bull returned to Standing Rock Agency in South Dakota. During an ensuing struggle between Sitting Bull's followers and the police, Sitting Bull was shot in the side and head by American police, after the police were fired upon by Sitting Bull's supporters. His body was taken to nearby Fort Yates for burial. He was born in 1831 and died in 1890.

There is also a large military cemetery on the grounds of the Little Bighorn National Monument for soldiers killed in all wars in which the U S Military has fought. Overall, visiting this was an unforgettable experience for us.

From there, we continued back into Wyoming on Interstate 90. Leaving the Little Big Horn in the late afternoon under perfect weather conditions and, with almost no traffic on I 90, we had one of the best rides of the entire trip. We rode **side by side,** better known as riding tandem, at 100 mph for over an hour, down the two eastbound lanes of Interstate 90. We were all alone, just the two of us, the highway, the deep blue sky above, rolling land that seemed to go on forever, the scent of dry sweet grasslands in the air and a warm wind on our faces. We felt in complete harmony with the universe. What a rush, life just doesn't get any better than that. The feel of the wind on our faces and the roar of the bikes was pure ecstasy. Things were really picking up. This is what biking and living is all about!

We arrived in Buffalo just before the sun set, found the Occidental Hotel (not hard), parked out front like the cowboys would have tied up their horses and checked in. Staying in the Occidental was a historic and scary experience. This Hotel, which has been open for over 125 years had, at various times in the past, housed a bordello and a 'speakeasy'. When we arrived, Dawn, the owner, gave us a big hug and let us have our choice of any room in the hotel. She invited us to go look around, check out any room with an open door and pick the room of our choice. Wow, this was different and fun. The original hotel was built around 1880 and had such famous people as

Butch Cassidy, the Sundance Kid, Buffalo Bill, President Theodore Roosevelt, Anny Oakley, members of the Hole-in-the-Wall Gang and Calamity Jane amongst others stay there. The hotel is authentic to its era in every way, the only things that are new are the mattresses on the beds. It's like spending a night in the 1880's. We got the royal treatment of dining in a special private room overlooking the main street, reminiscent of sitting in a display window with heavy velvet drapes, a beautiful authentic chandelier, velvet chairs matching the drapes, a creaky, well worn wooden floor and a waitress with stories of the unnatural events that have happened in the Hotel over the years. These stories included a private dinner party that had been held in the hotel, after which, when everyone had left the room, the dinner dishes were swept off the table onto the floor, where they broke. No staff member had been anywhere near the room, they just heard the noise of the dishes breaking.

After dinner we enjoyed a beer in the 1880 era Saloon. Of course, when you stay in a haunted hotel, something interesting is bound to happen. We can't really say we saw any ghosts that night but Roney got the scare of her life when she turned on the hot water tap in the old claw foot tub and the sound of rattling pipes could be heard down the hall. We were told we might see a young girl wondering around if we were really lucky (a footless ghost, of course). The following morning, Dawn gave us the grand tour of the hotel and told us about its history. Legend has it that some abortions were carried out here and the spirits of aborted babies may be the source of the ghosts. Apparently loud sad crying has kept some guests awake many nights and other strange noises have also been a problem. Dawn said it got so bad that she called the "Ghost Busters" to come in and stay the night to "put these souls to rest". Dawn said the Ghost Busters didn't make it through the night! They were last seen driving away with all speed from the hotel and refused to ever come back! Staying at the Occidental is like taking a time machine back to the days of the Wild West. We felt as though we could look out the window and see the Hole in the Wall Gang ride by at any moment.

Roney noticed a letter framed on the wall in the lower hall written by a lady who had worked at the hotel as a young woman. She was from Sundre, Alberta, Colin's home town. She'd written to apologize and pay for some spoons she had taken many years earlier when she worked there. The letter was written on March 19, 1951. Since Colin came from Sundre, we read the letter several times and decided to take down the name of the woman and ask a relative who still lives in Sundre if she knew of this woman. We later discovered that she was related to neighbours of Colin's family and that she had even worked for Colin's family at one time. Now that's a small world!

Ready to ride, April 29, 2007, Vancouver, B.C.

Checking out Virginia City, Montana

Visiting Old Faithful in Yellowstone National Park.

Buffalo along Highway 89 in Yellowstone National Park.

Snow banks along Highway 16 in Yellowstone National Park.

Roney in front of Buffalo Bill Museum, Cody, Wyoming

Little Big Horn National Monument and Military Cemetery, Crow Agency, Montana

The historic Occidental Hotel, Buffalo, Wyoming

CHAPTER 2 – EASTERN WYOMING TO NEW YORK

On Tuesday, May 8th, we left Buffalo, Wyoming under clear skies, heading east on Interstate 90, then north on Highway 14 at Moorcroft, WY then east on Highway 24 to Devil's Tower, **America's First National Monument.** Devils Tower is a very large Butte type rock formation with crevasses running down its full height. It is and always has been held in high esteem by Native Americans. Devils Tower was named America's first National Monument by President Theodore Roosevelt, the great naturalist, in 1906. The many columns that create Devils Tower can be 4, 5, 6, or 7 sided. Some geologists believe the last column collapsed 10,000 years ago. The Arapaho, Cheyenne, Crow, Kiowa, and Sioux Indians all have their own legends around this rock formation. Known to them as "Bears Tipi", it was later changed to Devils Tower. Even today, some Native Americans consider the area sacred, a place for prayer and renewal. We saw evidence of this on the bushes at the base of the butte, where they had left tokens and gifts. Devils Tower is also a popular climbing site. It is definitely worth seeing if you have the time.

After taking some photos and walking to the base of the monolith, we continued riding east on Highway 24, which changed to Highway 34 as we crossed the state line into South Dakota. We were now in prairie terrain, amid fields of grass and grain. The first order of business was to visit Sturgis, South Dakota, location of the annual Harley Davidson Rally. There's very little to see in Sturgis, other than during the H-D bike rally during the first week in August; just some bars, a casino, a restaurant called the **Road Kill Cafe,** several other businesses and a lumber mill. The Black Hill's roads south of Sturgis however, are legendary for motorcyclists.

Sturgis was named after Major Samuel D. Sturgis, a commander at local Fort Meade. Among other things, Major Sturgis lost a son during the Battle of Little Big Horn. The city of Sturgis itself was founded in the summer of 1876. Nearby Fort Meade became the training post for many regiments within the US army. Despite the amount of military traffic that came through the area during these initial years, it wasn't until the gold rush in the Black Hills that people started coming in large numbers. Three roads, intersecting at Bear Butte, brought travelers from Nebraska and North and South Dakota. Although the gold rush days are long gone, 6,682 people still call the Sturgis area home today. After taking several photos, we headed southeast on Interstate 90 to Rapid City then south on Highway 16 to Keystone, location of Mount Rushmore, within the Black Hills. We found a lovely Log House B&B called the Buffalo Rock **Lodge, with a view of Mount Rushmore and enjoyed a quiet night in a rural and quiet forested area.**

The next day, Wednesday May 9th, was again hot and sunny. After a hearty breakfast, we packed up and left Keystone and drove around Mount Rushmore to view the Presidents. Mount Rushmore was named after a New York attorney who visited the area in 1884, long before the statues were created. It is an incredible work of art, consisting of 4 past presidents, namely; George Washington, Thomas Jefferson, Abe Lincoln and Theodore Roosevelt.

"Mount Rushmore is a memorial that symbolizes America and Americans should never lose sight of their cultural beginnings." **Gerard Baker, Park Superintendent**

"The purpose of the memorial is to communicate the founding, expansion, preservation, and unification of the United States with colossal statues of Washington, Jefferson, Lincoln, and Theodore Roosevelt." **Gutzon Borglum, Sculptor**

Mount Rushmore is visited by almost three million people every year. It has grown in fame as a symbol of America, a symbol of freedom and hope for people from all cultures and backgrounds. After viewing Rushmore, we rode on to Biker Heaven. The roads in the Black Hills are among the best in North America, twisting and curling around themselves, crossing narrow bridges and through single lane tunnels. The Black Hills are an oasis of pine-clad mountains on the Great Plains, a place where bison and wild horses still roam free. The Black Hills offer everything you could expect from a national forest; scenic drives, waterfalls, abundant wildlife, acclaimed recreation trails and trout fishing. After taking photos, we headed south from the Black Hills, passing the "Crazy Horse Monument", which is being created by Native Americans to commemorate one of their leaders.

At this point, we knew we wanted to head south to go around the bottom of the Great Lakes, so after Roney bought a Sturgis T-shirt and leather backpack in Custer, SD; we departed South Dakota on Highway 385 to Pringle and crossed into Nebraska. We rode southeast on Highway 385 for a couple of hours through Alliance and onto Bridgeport, where we picked up US Highway 26, which parallels the old Oregon Trail and the North Platt River. This section of the Oregon Trail was traversed by the Lewis and Clark expedition in 1804 and became one of the main overland migration routes on the North American continent, leading from the Missouri River to the Oregon Territory. The eastern half of the trail was also used by travelers going to on the California and Bozeman Trails. Between 1841 and 1869 this section of the Oregon Trail was used by the Mormons during their great exodus to the Salt Lake Valley and by numerous settlers, miners and business men migrating to the Pacific Northwest United States.

We rode Highway 26 until it intersected with Interstate 80 at Ogallala, Nebraska, where we fueled up. From there, we rode east until we got close to North Platt, by which time it was twilight, and we left the freeway to find a B&B we had booked earlier. It was dark by this time and without a street address, our GPS was of little use. We phoned the B&B again to get directions and then started down a dirt road topped with 4" of loose sand and gravel. Cruiser Motorcycles are not made for this type of road, which we discovered to our dismay after we had gone about 100 yards down this road! There was no option of turning around, and shortly Colin lost control of his bike (at less than 5 MPH) and dumped into Roney and down we both went. Fortunately, we suffered no physical injuries, (Roney's shinny new bike was no longer shinny – you could say the air was a little blue!), so without saying too much to each other we got the bikes up, checked them out and kept going, as we didn't have any other option. Colin almost dumped again but managed to stay up, unfortunately Roney got into deeper sand where a driveway entered the road and when Colin looked back she was down on the road with her bike on top of her! Colin ran back to help, not knowing she was knocked out. Luckily for us, a man named Chuck, from a nearby farm, seeing what had happened, had run out and helped Roney up. She was pretty shaken up and had to rest until we got her bike up and off the main part of the road. This time the highway bar on her bike was bent and the bike wouldn't go into gear, however the highway bar had saved Roney's leg from injury, so it had done its job. Chuck made sure we were okay and then had a look to see if he could fix Roney's bike (he used to ride motorcycles and now raises Arabian horses). The highway bar had been pushed back onto the gear shift pedal, jamming it. We pushed Roney's bike into his horse barn, which excited the beautiful Arabian horses inside and, using a 2 X 4, we managed to straighten the crash bar so that the bike could be driven. We also noticed that her front fender was broken. After we admired his beautiful horses, he got his wife up (it was late by this time and his wife was asleep) and he rode Roney's bike a few miles until we reached pavement while his wife followed with Roney in their pickup. He advised us not to use B&Bs in Nebraska as they are almost always on bad rural roads. He told us that he and his neighbours had been fighting with the County for a long time to improve their road without success. That night, we stayed in a hotel just off the freeway in North Platt.

Thursday May 10th, was another hot and sunny day. We reported the previous day's accident to the local County Sherriff, who took a report and photos of the damage, but they took no responsibility for road conditions. Colin took Roney's bike to the Kawasaki dealer in North Platt where he was assured that the bike was safe to drive, it just had some scrapes and needed a new highway bar, which they did not have in stock, so we just removed the damaged one. We left North Platt and continued east on Interstate 80. We made excellent time, stopping only for gas and eats, riding through to Council Bluffs, Iowa, where we stayed the night. Riding in Nebraska is just about the same as riding in Iowa or southern Saskatchewan and Manitoba, long stretches of straight highway with everyone driving like hell. Iowa seems to consist of endless fields and flatland, however we realized that this is the Heartland of America as well as America's Breadbasket and recognized that it has its own special beauty.

Friday May 11th We were happy to be experiencing a shift in the weather to hot and sunny, just what we were looking for. We left Council Bluffs, Iowa about 9.00 am and rode until 5.00 pm on Interstate 80 until we reached Morris, Illinois, which is about 50 miles west of Chicago. We only stopped three times for gas, once to eat and to stretch our legs in Des Moines, Waukee and Williamsburg. I followed Roney most of the day and the girl can ride!! Her motto is if you can't see through it, around it or over it then pass it so you know what is going on ahead of you. We spent the day passing semis, two groups of motorcycles and lots of cars. Riding on those straight fast roads in Iowa requires full attention as, with minimal curves, hills or mountains, there is little of interest to see and falling asleep is a real possibility. We travelled 382 miles and felt very tired by the end of the day. We over nighted in Morris, Illinois and planned a long trip the next day as our first time-share week was scheduled to start on Sunday, May 13th at Catskill, New York, two days away.

Saturday May 12th started out partly overcast but cleared up by mid-morning. We left Morris, Illinois at 7.30 am, after a fast breakfast and rode hard. We rode in 5 states that day, the longest one day run of our entire trip. Starting in Illinois, we rode around the south side of Chicago on Interstate 90, which we cleared before 8.30 am. We noticed the interstate was under major repair and we had to watch signage very closely and we really glad we started out so early in the morning. We rode across Indiana, where we stopped for gas in Howe, IN, then across Ohio where we stopped to eat and twice for gas in Genoa, OH and in Cleveland, OH (we saw Indian Stadium from the freeway). We continued on through the northern corner of Pennsylvania and on into New York State, where we turned east onto Interstate 86. This area of upstate New York was hilly and scenic. We stopped for the night at a hotel in Jamestown, NY, just off Interstate 86. A very noisy air conditioner somewhere nearby kept us from getting a good night's sleep but we were too tired to move to another part of the hotel (once you unpack your bike and put everything in your room you think twice about moving to another room in the middle of the night). Somehow we did finally get a little sleep just before dawn. The next morning we complained and got our stay for free!

We left Jamestown on Sunday May 13th, continuing on Interstate 86 headed for Catskill, New York. The weather was absolutely perfect. Things were getting better and better. We rode about 100 miles and stopped for gas in Belmont, NY where, to our dismay, we discovered that Roney's gas tank was leaking fuel just above the fuel injection pump. We tried to find the source of the leak as did a couple of other people that stopped for gas and offered to help; however we were not able find it or get it fixed. Belmont has no bike shop and the local mechanic was unable to help and, being a Sunday didn't help either. Part of the front fender of Roney's bike was still there from our accident in Nebraska, so Colin broke a sizeable piece off and jury rigged it as a deflector so that the gas would fall onto the broken fender and then drain away from the bike. Thank God for duct tape. We had no other choice and carried on to our destination with Colin riding Roney's bike and her riding Colin's bike. It was a stressful ride from where this happened to Catskill, NY, a distance of about 200 miles but we made it. We called ahead to a dealer near our timeshare and left a message with them to make arrangements to have the bike serviced so we would have someone to fix it for us or order a new tank if necessary. We arrived at the time-share resort around 8.00 pm. Colin was pretty happy to get off the Kawasaki and away from that ever present gas leak, which was like riding a Molotov Cocktail, but at least now we could get the bike repaired, take some down time and visit the Big Apple.

Devils Tower National Monument, Wyoming

Main Street, Sturgis, South Dakota, home of the annual Harley Davidson rally during the first week of August each year. Just another quiet little town the other 51 weeks of the year.

Rushmore National Monument, Keystone, South Dakota

Sundown on the Prairie, Highway 26, Nebraska

Roney riding across the mighty Mississippi

Chapter 3 – New York

Monday, May 14th   Our time-share Resort, the "Nottingham Village at Friar Tuck" near Catskill State Park, is a very unusual resort and rather out of the way. It was built in a picturesque location on a large tract of land, complete with ponds, pools and beautiful shade trees edging acres of cleared grass land, also beautiful gardens everywhere. The resort looked like a medieval castle with several motel like rows of rooms nearby. The inside of the lobby contained simulated antiques of King Arthur's time period complete with very heavy red velvet drapes, over stuffed couches and chairs, a huge fireplace and large rough black beams on the white ceilings. It was built as a resort theme destination and conference center with a quaint gift shop in the lower "dungeon" area. There are many hallways that seem to go on forever, ballrooms and even two large indoor swimming pools. Unfortunately, there were no stores nearby to purchase groceries or any restaurants other than one inside the "castle", so we ate there. Sadly it did not meet our expectation and as we looked around and chatted with some of the staff we discovered that the whole resort was sadly in need of major repairs but because it was not "in vogue" anymore the current owner was just letting things run their course. We had quite a time finding it in the dark last night and were not prepared to be so isolated. However, at least it gave us a warm and dry place to stay while the Kawasaki fuel leak was repaired. Any trip has its trials and with ingenuity and duct tape we were able to rise to the challenge. We were happy that we had a down time week here to sightsee, visit NYC, do laundry and just read and relax.

After a good night's rest, we did some exploring of the local Hudson Valley area in and around our resort looking for a place to have breakfast, then set out to find Matt's Honda shop. Then the surprise, Roney's New Kawasaki warranty would not be honoured in the USA as Kawasaki Canada and Kawasaki USA are different companies. A new tank was required because the leak was on a seam of the tank and a new one had to be ordered in. Of course this would take a few days to arrive and be installed, so it was a doubly good thing that we had a week to spare. We learned that we would have to pay for the repairs on the Kawasaki, even though it was under warranty, then make a claim when we returned home. Also, Kawasaki's delivered in Canada only have Kilometers displayed on their speedometers, so Roney had to 'guess' her speeds which, of course, are posted in Miles Per Hour throughout the USA. We left Roney's Kawasaki with the dealer and rode two-up on the Honda, getting lost a couple of times in the process but enjoying the local scenery and the warm weather. We decided then to start using Martha, our GPS Mapping unit, wow, what a difference. No more getting lost. Roney had lost her glasses 'somewhere in Nebraska' during our adventures there, so we sought out a local optical shop and ordered a new pair of prescription glasses and more contact lenses. After a visit to the local library to send home our weekly update to family and friends, we headed back to the resort and had a quiet evening in.

On Tuesday May 15th, we decided we would take an Amtrak train into New York City. The only way to do this was to leave both bikes with the Kawasaki/Honda dealer while we were in New York. We went to the AAA office in Hudson and spent more than an hour with a wonderful travel agent, who finally found us a postage stamp sized room in NYC for less than $300.00 per night. We also bought Mets tickets (we just missed out on the annual Yankee/Mets Subway Series Game). After returning to the resort, we had dinner and packed a small bag of clothes for our New York City adventure the following day.

Wednesday, May 16th   We got up early and took the Honda to Matt's Honda for service, and then took the one and only local taxi to the Hudson City Amtrak Station. We left for New York at 8.30 am and arrived at Penn Station at 10.30 am. We learned that the railway station in Hudson was one of the oldest in the United States, through which many troops travelled back and forth during the Civil War. The trip along the Hudson River Valley was something to behold. There are many large and stately homes, some looking like castles including one on an island. It was a photographer's delight! Once in New York City we went immediately to Times Square. It is a very humbling experience to stand there looking up at all the billboards that apparently make millions of dollars per week advertising products. There are so many huge billboards and the lights are just incredible, especially at night. Everywhere you look you are just in awe! New York City is something to behold. There are over 800 languages spoken in New York. We had trouble taking it all in. We walked to the subway, which we took to our Hotel, in Manhattan. We shoehorned our way into our room at the Comfort Inn, which Roney renamed the 'Compact Inn'. It turned out several Universities were graduating thousands of students and the hotels were filled with families and friends, in addition to the normal tourists and conference goers. Most were going to graduation ceremonies at Columbia University. That afternoon, we went to a matinee Play on Broadway called "Journey's End", set in a British trench and bunker during World War 1. We had no time to eat before going to the show and the theatre was full so we had to eat chocolate bars very quietly because you could have heard a pin drop. The weather was wonderful when we went into the theater, but when we came out, it was pouring. We went for dinner, then took the Subway to Queens to see the Mets game at Shea Stadium, hoping it wouldn't be rain cancelled. Shea Stadium is located in Queens in an area that is not very appealing; Roney was a little apprehensive about walking around when we got off the train. We arrived at the Stadium in the pouring rain, found our seats, which weren't covered, and waited under cover with several thousand other fans to see if the game against the Chicago Cubs would be played. After an hour and a half of rain and no sign of letting up, people began leaving and said we could get our money back the next day if the game had to be cancelled. We went back to our hotel and with the intent of getting a refund the next day. Well, on our way back to our hotel, the rain stopped in Queens, even though it was still pouring in down town New York, so the game was played without us. Too bad so sad for us! Obviously we are meant to go back to New York when the Yankees and Mets are playing!

On Thursday May 17th, we decided to do the "topless" bus tour of uptown & downtown Manhattan and had the busiest day during the entire trip. Before the tour, we went downtown and explored Trump Tower, where Roney bought a necklace and I bought a Trump Towers golf shirt. Then we went to 5th Avenue, the famous shopping district, where Roney bought a pair of very elegant gold twist earrings from Tiffany's! They go so well with her jeans and black leather riding clothes! After that, we bought a new digital camera and, within a block, ended up in front of a hotel where some of the cast from "House" were emerging. There were a number of people milling around and lots of Security and Limos. We watched for about 45 minutes and recognized several actors, but couldn't put names to them. Roney played Paparazzi and got lots of shots. There were so many people pushing and shoving to get in position for "the perfect" picture that a woman dropped two bottles of wine she had in a brown paper bag, which broke and dumped red wine all over the sidewalk. She just looked at the poor hotel staff that came out to clean up the mess and said "Well if you had allowed me to be at the front of the line this would not have happened, so I think you should replace the two bottles of wine for me". Needless to say the poor hotel staff did not say a thing and cleaned up the broken glass and the wine as best as they could. ONLY IN NEW YORK!

We decided to go to another Play, bought 1/2 price tickets at a kiosk at the Marriott, where half price tickets are sold for same day shows, when available. Needless to say the lines are long and a little confusing as there are separate lines for each specific show. After purchasing our tickets, we took the double decker bus tour, which was great. It's a typical hop on hop off loop; we got off and went up the Empire State Building, where we took lots of shots of the skyline. We went past Rockefeller Centre, Radio City Music Hall, Madison Square Gardens and the United Nations Headquarters.

We visited the site of the World Trade Centre, which was then a huge construction zone. The site was hardly mentioned in the commentary on the tour bus and was really down played as a point of interest. We understand the sadness and loss but we felt that it was a "must see", so we went back later on our own.

We were a little disappointed that the World Trade Centre Site still did not have a befitting memorial to the many people who died there. What did exist was of a very temporary nature; however we're sure that something very special will be placed on this site as reminder of how precious and important our freedom is. We would certainly like to see a tribute to the many Firefighters and Police Officers, and other people who gave their lives to save and help others that were hurt, disoriented and who suffered posttraumatic stress syndrome from the experience. Those that rushed to the two towers after they were initially hit by the airliners had to know that they were risking their lives and there is no greater sacrifice one can make than that! Having visited the Site, we came away with a greater appreciation of the events that happened and how those events changed all of our lives forever. We think it's safe to say that we, in the Western World, and particularly, the United States of America, lost our innocence on 9/11. It brought the war against terrorism right here at home, not just on TV or countries that we may never see! How sobering is that! It was a very moving experience to stand on that site. Like the assassination of President J.F. Kennedy, seeing those buildings being hit by airliners and then seeing them collapse was one we shall never forget. The best and the worst of mankind were on display on September 11, 2001. The Trade Centre Towers were actually relatively new to NYC. Ground was broken in August, 1966, they were completed and opened in April, 1973 and destroyed on September 11, 2001. We later learned that the medical system was not going to pay for people who volunteered at Ground Zero and who felt that they had respiratory ailments from inhaling the dust and fumes, conditions resulting from events that dreadful day, which is very sad. At the same time, suspected terrorists, sworn enemies of our way of life, were receiving free medical treatment while in custody at Guantanamo Bay; sometimes our priorities seem completely out of whack!

We went to the waterfront to see the Statute of Liberty, which was larger than we expected and where we learned some of the history behind its creation. The story of it's creation is a very interesting one, one which we want to share with you. The sculptor, who designed the Statue of Liberty, Frédéric-Auguste Bartholdi, was born into a well-to-do family in Colmar, France on August 2, 1834. He was introduced to the idea of a statue in New York Harbor, to symbolize the place "where people would get their first view of the New World", by Edouard Laboulaye, a French scholar. He saw Bedloe's Island, in the middle of New York Harbor, as the ideal spot during a trip to America. The island was federal territory and was located just opposite the Narrows, which are, so to speak, the gateway to America.

Intelligent, warm, persuasive and charming, Bartholdi impressed the many prominent Americans he met, including President Ulysses S. Grant, Henry Wadsworth Longfellow, Horace Greeley and Senator Charles Sumner. He traveled across America, which filled him with amazement. He wrote, "Everything in America is big ... Here, even the peas are big." Everywhere he went, he enthusiastically promoted his sketch and a model he carried of the statue as it would appear on the island in New York Harbor. Americans seemed receptive to the idea of a statue dedicated to "Liberty Enlightening the World" (the official name for the statue), but no one was willing to make a commitment of money or a building site. Upon his return to France, Bartholdi completed other projects, all the while refining his ideas and design for "the American statue."

In 1875, with the establishment of the Third Republic, Edouard Laboulaye, a scholar and originator of the idea of the statue to commemorate the alliance between France and America during the War of Independence, joined with Bartholdi to create the statue. Because the project would be extremely expensive, they decided its cost should be shared: France would pay for the statue; America would pay for its pedestal and foundation. A fund-raising committee called the Franco-American Union was formed with members from both nations. Elaborate fund-raising events were staged, but money was slow coming in. Enough was collected to begin work on the statue, but the goal of completing it in time for America's 100th anniversary in 1876 was impossible.

Bartholdi selected Gaget, Gauthier and Company as the foundry where the sculpture was to be constructed. Its craftsmen were experts in the art of repoussé, a technique for creating sculptural forms by hammering sheet metal inside molds. Lighter than casting metal, repoussé was the only method available that would allow such a monumental work to be shipped overseas. The intricate skeleton for the statue was designed by famed engineer Alexandre-Gustave Eiffel, already known for his brilliant iron railroad bridges and later, the Eiffel Tower. Bartholdi was chosen as an official French representative to the International Centennial Exhibition in Philadelphia in 1876. With three major sculptures on view at the Exhibition, Bartholdi's name was becoming known in America.

The 30-foot arm of Liberty traveled to Philadelphia in 1876. For 50 cents visitors could climb a steel ladder to the balcony around the torch. A good deal of enthusiasm was generated for the project, since Liberty would be the first statue one could climb inside.

When Liberty's gleaming copper head appeared at the fair, she was a sensation. She wasn't sensational enough, however, to solve the never-ending problem of raising the money to complete her construction. Someone with the Franco-American Union had an inspiration; they would hold a lottery. Since very few contributions were coming from France's moneyed elite, the idea of engaging the public's attention with a lottery was a brilliant one. The prizes were highly coveted and valuable, including two works by Bartholdi himself. Additional funds were raised in a manner worthy of contemporary merchandising techniques: a signed and numbered collection of clay models of the statue were sold in France and America. By the end of 1879, about 250,000 francs (approximately $750,000 U.S.) had been raised for the statue's construction. Enough, most people thought, to complete the work.

In May 1883, Laboulaye died of a heart ailment, never to see his dream come to life. At last, in June 1884, Liberty received her final touches. She was dedicated with much pomp and circumstance by French Prime Minister Jules Ferry and Ambassador Morton. But when Bartholdi invited the celebrating party to join him in climbing the statue's steps, few accepted the challenge. Until the spring of 1885, when she was dismantled for the long voyage to America, Liberty remained in Paris, hostess to thousands of French visitors.

While the statue was nearing completion in France, little was happening on the American side. The American press continued to be critical of the project, especially of its cost. They couldn't understand why the pedestal should cost as much as the statue itself. Congress rejected a bill appropriating $100,000 for the base. New York approved a grant of $50,000, but the expenditure was vetoed by the governor. Many Americans outside of New York considered it New York's statue. "Let New York pay for it," they said, while America's newly rich, self-made millionaires were saying and contributing nothing. The American half of the Franco-American Union, led by William M. Evarts, held the usual fund-raising events, but public apathy was almost as monumental as the statue itself.

By 1884, after years of fund-raising, only $182,491 had been collected and $179,624 had been spent. It took the intervention of Joseph Pulitzer and the power of the media to make a difference. Joseph Pulitzer was a Hungarian immigrant who fought in the Civil War, became a successful journalist and married a wealthy woman. In 1883, he bought a financial newspaper called the *World*; he already owned the *St. Louis Post-Dispatch*. When he heard that the Statue of Liberty was about to die from lack of funds, he saw his chance to take advantage of three distinct opportunities: to raise funds for the statue, to increase his newspaper's circulation and to blast the rich for their selfishness.

Pulitzer set the fund-raising goal of the *World* at $100,000. In its pages he taunted the rich, thereby increasing the paper's appeal among working-class people, and firmly planted the notion that the statue was a monument not just for New York City but, indeed, for all of America. Perhaps Pulitzer's cleverest ploy was the promise to publish the name of every single contributor in the pages of the *World*, no matter how small the contribution. The editorial that opened the fund-raising campaign set its tone. He wrote: "The *World* is the people's paper and it now appeals to the people to come forward and raise the money for the statue's pedestal." The statue, he said, was paid for by "The masses of the French people. Let us respond in like manner to pay for its base. Let us not wait for the millionaires to give this money. It is not a gift from the millionaires of France to the millionaires of America, but a gift of the whole people of France to the whole people of America." The circulation of the *World* increased by almost 50,000 copies. African American newspapers joined in the effort, encouraging their readers to contribute to a monument that would, in part, commemorate the end of slavery. So the money poured in, with single-dollar donations from grandmothers and pennies from the piggybanks of schoolchildren. On June 15, 1885, the Statue of Liberty arrived at Bedloe's Island inside 214 wooden packing crates.

On August 11, 1885, the front page of the *World* proclaimed, "ONE HUNDRED THOUSAND DOLLARS!" The goal had been reached, and slightly exceeded, thanks to more than 120,000 contributions.

The architect for Liberty's pedestal, Richard Morris Hunt, was a highly respected and popular designer of expensive homes. He designed the 89-foot-high pedestal that would sit upon a concrete foundation that would appear to grow up from within the 11-pointed, star-shaped walls of the existing Fort Wood. His fee for the project was $1,000, which he returned to the fund to reassemble the statue.

General Charles P. Stone was the chief engineer in charge of the entire construction project, including the foundation, the pedestal and the reassembly of the statue. Liberty's foundation alone required 24,000 tons of concrete, the largest single mass ever poured at that time. It measures 52 feet, 10 inches in height. At the bottom, it is 91 feet, and at the top, it is 65 feet. The Statue of Liberty began to rise over her new home in America in May of 1886. It would take six months to mount the statue to her base. On October 25, 1886, Bartholdi and his wife, accompanied by Viscount Ferdinand-Marie de Lesseps, chairman of the Franco-American Union, arrived in America. They were greeted by the American Committee and Joseph Pulitzer. At Bedloe's Island, surrounded by newspaper reporters recording his words for posterity, Bartholdi simply said, "The dream of my life is accomplished."

Unveiling day, October 28, 1886, was declared a public holiday. The rainy, foggy day could not dampen the spirits of the more than 1 million people who lined New York's streets, draped with red, white and blue and French tricolor bunting, to watch a parade of more than 20,000 pass by. Wall Street was the only area of the city working on the day of Liberty's unveiling. The New York Times reported that as the parade passed by, the office boys "from a hundred windows began to unreel spools of tape, thus creating the 'ticker tape parade.' In a moment the air was white with curling streamers."

Dignitaries from both nations were in attendance. Representing America were President Grover Cleveland and his cabinet as well as the governor of New York and his staff. The French ambassador attended, accompanied by the French Committee. And, most ironically, members of some of America's wealthiest families - the same families who had not contributed a single cent to the statue's pedestal - now jockeyed for seats of prominence. New York, reported the *World*, "was one vast cheer."

Out on the water, the fog rolled in and out. The harbor teemed with ships of all sizes. Bartholdi stood alone in the head of the statue. He was to pull a cord that would drop the French tricolor veil from the face of the statue. For his cue, Bartholdi was to watch for a signal from a boy on the ground below, who would wave a handkerchief. The signal would come when Senator William M. Evarts, considered one of the more talented orators of his time, finished his presentation speech.

Evarts began his speech, stopped momentarily to take a breath, and the boy, thinking the speech was over, gave Bartholdi the signal. Bartholdi pulled the cord, revealing the statue's gleaming copper face to the world. Whistles blasted, guns roared, bands played and Evarts sat down.

When it was President Cleveland's turn to speak, he said, "We will not forget that Liberty has made her home here, nor shall her chosen altar be neglected." At the time of the Statue of Liberty's dedication, she was the tallest structure in New York, reaching a total height of 305 feet. It wasn't until 1899 that she was overtaken by Saint Paul's Building, which rose to 310 feet. Lady Liberty remains the visual and inspirational center of New York Harbor.

In 1903, one of the most memorable changes to the statue occurred without fanfare or publicity. A bronze tablet was fastened to an interior wall of the pedestal. Cast as a part of the plaque was a poem written in 1883 that has become the credo for thousands of immigrants coming to America. The poem, "The New Colossus," was written by Emma Lazarus to help raise funds for the construction of the statue's pedestal. Today, many people think of the statue and poem as inseparable. In 1916, the *World* once again raised its voice to raise funds on behalf of the statue. This time, the goal was to floodlight the statue at night. The paper's readers contributed $30,000 and the torch was also redesigned in glass.

From the time of the Revolutionary War, the female figure Columbia was generally regarded as the symbol for America, but the statue's increased visibility and popularity during World War I easily shifted America's symbolic loyalties. Liberty's features appeared everywhere; she became a kind of female equivalent to Uncle Sam. To help finance U.S. participation in the war, the Treasury Department authorized using the statue as a rallying symbol on posters designed to raise funds. The government sold about $15 billion worth of bonds, equal to about half the cost of World War I. President Calvin Coolidge declared the Statue of Liberty to be a national monument on October 15, 1924. In 1933, the National Park Service took over its administration and maintenance.

Another famous landmark of New York Harbour is Ellis Island, the first place new Immigrants, mostly from Europe, set foot in the "New World". Immigrants arriving by ship went through their screening process here before being allowed to enter New York City. While looking at the buildings there, we wondered how many thousands and thousands of people had stood looking from that vantage point towards New York City, awaiting clearance to enter. They were the poor and dispossessed looking for the country where anything and everything was possible. A large number of the current population of the United States can trace their roots back to immigrants that passed through Ellis Island. Ellis Island was used for immigration purposes from 1892 through 1954, clearing an estimated 12,000,000 people.

Later in our trip, we were to discover that many men entering the USA through the Port of New York during the Civil War, who had high hopes of a better future, were enlisted into the Union Army when they arrived. Upon arrival to the US of A they were given papers to fill out with their name, country of origin and family members. Along with these papers, the men, in some cases unknowingly, filled out papers that said they had enlisted in the army and were told to "sign here" and say goodbye to their families, as now they were in the fight against the South in the Civil War. After fighting in the Civil War, a few of these very men died at the Battle of The Little Big Horn and never saw their families again after landing on the shores of the United States. We all know the stories from history and movies of the shantytowns that were formed in New York by the families that arrived by ship during that period of time. Those that could not get work were disheartened, starving and wondering what would become of them. They couldn't go back home and would have been worse off there, in what they called the "old country". Many people formed into ethnic groups and that was how the different parts of New York were started.

A newspaper headline on Tuesday July 22, 2008 stated:

NEW YORK -- Mayor Michael Bloomberg ordered city agencies today to offer services in the six most common foreign languages spoken in New York City: Spanish, Chinese, Russian, Korean, Italian and French Creole.
This illustrates the multi-cultural makeup of New York City.

After the bus tour, we grabbed two chocolate bars each for dinner and went straight to our Broadway Play called Deuce, staring Angela Lansbury (of Murder She Wrote). It was a play about two women who were famous tennis players and how aging and growing old had affected them both personally and professionally. There was also a live play down the street on 44th staring Vanessa Redgrave and another play in a theatre across the street with Christopher Plummer. We bought tickets for the play "Grease" to see on our next visit in the fall en route to South Africa. After the show, we went up to a revolving restaurant to eat a typical "after theatre snack complete with champagne and chocolate desserts" and then went to experience Times Square at night. Believe it or not the sidewalks were even busier at night than in the daytime. The people of New York were great, much more friendly and helpful than most large cities and most have a great sense of humour. If we asked for directions people were more than courteous and helpful. We can't say enough about NYC and the people. Any style of clothes can be seen there and anything can be purchased there. It is a shopper's paradise. It really is bigger than life. We're looking forward to returning again in the future.

The next morning, Friday May 18th, we checked out of the **Compact Inn,** said goodbye to our postage stamp sized room then went to see Grand Central Station. Then it was off to Penn Station and back by train to Hudson, where our taxi driver picked us up in a **30 passenger school bus,** because the one taxi was not running that day. We should have taxi drivers like him at home. We got a great tour of the area, including info on the Vanderbilt, Rothschild's and Roosevelt homes (mansions that looked like castles) and, bonus; he could even speak perfect English. He returned us to our Kawasaki/Honda dealer where both bikes were ready to go. After picking up Roney's new glasses and contacts, we returned to the resort and had dinner in (hamburgers - <u>underdone</u>).

What memories we now had of the Big Apple. We talked most of the night about the sights, smells, and experiences we had just had. New York City is probably the world's most cosmopolitan city, its residents come from everywhere, speak most of the world's major language groups. It is a place everyone should visit at least once in their lifetime.

On our last day at the time-share resort, Saturday May 19th, it rained all day. We spent most of the day indoors packing, reading, doing laundry and sleeping. It was great to be caught up on our laundry, but now came the problem of where to put everything we had magically acquired on the trip so far. Loading up the bikes to leave the next day was going to be an even greater challenge so we decided to send home the first box of clothes we would no longer need. This idea turned out to be an absolute blessing, one which we repeated throughout our trip.

This is a unique photo of the top portion of one of the Trade Centre towers just before they collapsed. There were 2974 innocent people confirmed dead that dreadful day. Most were civilians, some were nationals from 90 different countries. The buildings collapsed within two hours of being struck by the two airliners, a sight none of us shall ever forget.

Roney atop the Empire State Building, NYC, New York

Evening in Times Square, New York City

Gettysburg National Historic Site, Pennsylvania

The historic Brafferton Inn B & B, Gettysburg, Pennsylvania

Chapter 4 – Gettysburg, PA, Washington DC and Virginia

Sunday May 20th, check out day at our New York resort, started out cloudy, then cleared up around 11.00 am, just about the time we left the Resort. We headed south on Interstate 87 in the direction of New York City, then turned west onto Interstate 84, then onto Interstate 81 headed for Gettysburg via Harrisburg, PA. We share a common interest in the Civil War and had planned part of our explorations around various Civil War sites and going to a Civil War Reenactment. Despite many hours surfing the net before we left Victoria looking for a Reenactment somewhere along our intended routes, we had been unable to find any during our time in the south. At any rate, we intended to see as many Civil War Sites as possible. Little did we know at this time how lucky we were going to be throughout the rest of our ride.

By the time we fueled up, the skies were completely clear and the riding was fantastic. This area of the Northeast is really beautiful, made up of rolling hills and forests. In Harrisburg, the capitol of Pennsylvania, we turned south onto Highway 15 and headed into Gettysburg and checked into a B&B called the Brafferton Inn. It is the longest continuous operating Inn in Gettysburg, pre-existing the Civil War. The room we stayed in was very period. It had a fireplace in the corner with a lead ball still embedded in the mantel, supposedly from the great battle. No word on whether it was a Union or Confederate lead ball, but I guess that doesn't matter, as both were equally deadly. We went for a walk and found a lovely small pub for dinner then walked the town square, which was much the same as it had been during the Civil War. We had ridden about 200 miles that day and passed through or around places such as Bushville, Matamoras, Warrior Run, McAdoo, Frackville, East Hanover, Dillsburg, York Springs and Brush Run. Our room and the street outside our window probably looked the same at the time of the battle at Gettysburg.

The **Battle of Gettysburg** (July 1–3, 1863) was fought in and around the town of Gettysburg, Pennsylvania, as part of the Gettysburg Campaign. This was the battle with the largest number of casualties during the American Civil War and it is frequently cited as the war's turning point. Union Maj. Gen. George Gordon Meade's Army of the Potomac defeated attacks by Confederate Gen. Robert E. Lee's Army of Northern Virginia, ending Lee's invasion of the North. Following his success at Chancellorsville in May 1863, Lee led his army through the Shenandoah Valley for his second invasion of the North, hoping to reach as far as Harrisburg, PA, or even Philadelphia, and to influence Northern politicians to give up their prosecution of the war. Prodded by President Abraham Lincoln, Maj. Gen. Joseph Hooker moved his army in pursuit, but was relieved just three days before the battle and replaced by Meade.

The two armies began to collide at Gettysburg on July 1, 1863, as Lee urgently concentrated his forces there. Low ridges to the northwest of town were defended initially by a Union cavalry division, which was soon reinforced with two corps of Union infantry. However, two large Confederate corps assaulted them from the northwest and collapsed the hastily developed Union lines, sending the defenders retreating through the streets of town to the hills just to the south.

On the second day of battle, most of both armies had assembled. The Union line was laid out in a defensive formation resembling a fishhook. Lee launched a heavy assault on the Union left flank, and fierce fighting raged at Little Round Top, the Wheatfield, Devil's

Den, and the Peach Orchard. On the Union right, full-scale assaults on Culp's Hill and Cemetery Hill took place. Across the battlefield, despite significant losses, the Union defenders held their lines.

On the third day of battle, July 3, fighting resumed on Culp's Hill, and cavalry battles raged to the east and south, but the main event was a dramatic infantry assault by 12,500 Confederates against the center of the Union line on Cemetery Ridge. Pickett's Charge was repulsed by Union rifle and artillery fire at great losses to the Confederate army. Lee led his army on a torturous retreat back to Virginia. Between 46,000 and 51,000 Americans were casualties in the three-day battle.

Union casualties were 23,055 (3,155 killed, 14,531 wounded, 5,369 captured or missing). Confederate casualties were estimated at (4,708 killed, 12,693 wounded, 5,830 captured or missing). There was one documented civilian death during the battle; Ginnie Wade, 20 years old, was shot by a stray bullet that passed through her kitchen in town while she was making bread. Nearly 8,000 had been killed outright; these bodies, lying in the hot summer sun, needed to be buried quickly. Over 3,000 horse carcasses were burned in a series of piles south of town; townsfolk became violently ill from the stench. The ravages of war would still be evident in Gettysburg more than four months later when, on November 19, the Soldiers' National Cemetery was dedicated. During this ceremony, President Abraham Lincoln, in his famous Gettysburg Address, re-dedicated the Union to the war effort. Today, the Gettysburg National Cemetery and Gettysburg National Military Park are maintained by the U.S. National Park Service as two of the nation's most revered historical landmarks.

Monday, May 21st   We are just starting our fourth week and already we've put on some 3500 miles since leaving home. Our first full day in Gettysburg was wonderfully sunny. The Brafferton B&B, where we are staying, was built in 1786, just 10 years after the US War of Independence and 75 years before the start of the Civil War. The Town of Gettysburg is very historic and the citizens there have done a great job of keeping the downtown core much as it did at the time of the Civil War. Many of the buildings are 150 years old and some as many as 200 years old. We wandered the town, looked in a lot of shops, and then we went to see the Gettysburg Battlefield National Monument and Cemetery. More soldiers from both sides were killed, injured or missing at Gettysburg than at any other battle of the Civil War. The National Historic Site building contains an impressive audio/visual presentation of the Battle. We also went to the site where Abe Lincoln gave his famous Gettysburg address.

We met an interesting woman working in the information center that was very knowledgeable about the Civil War and the events leading up to it. While the major reason for the Civil War involved abolishing slavery (emancipation), it also involved taxes. The major crop from the South was cotton, much of which was shipped to Europe. When the European merchants paid for their shipments, Washington collected duties. The South was primarily an agricultural economy, while the North was primarily industrial. The North also had a larger population than the south. Many Southerners felt that they were being unfairly taxed – taxation without representation - as more money was spent on the North than the South. Hence, taxation by Washington of Southern crops also contributed to the Southern States succeeding from the Union. Once succession began and the first shot was fired upon Fort Sumter, the War was underway and the North quickly "blockaded" the South, effectively cutting them off from the rest of the World. In the meantime, the North outnumbered the South and also had a steady stream of immigrants arriving, mostly through New York. The male immigrants were made American Citizens and were then drafted into the Union Army, trained, armed and sent to the front, wherever that happened to be. Meanwhile, in the South, the Confederate Army had to enlist from the existing male population. Also, some Northerners also had slaves until Abraham Lincoln signed the Emancipation Act. So, while slavery was certainly an important aspect of the Civil War, it certainly was not the only reason why the War was fought. It is interesting to note that more Americans died during the course of the Civil War than all other Wars that America has fought before or since (including the Revolutionary War, the War of 1812, the Mexican War, the First and Second World Wars, Korea, Vietnam, the First Gulf War, Iraq and Afghanistan wars). That is a pretty incredible statistic, until you consider that every soldier killed or wounded, from both sides, were Americans. This, of course, only happens during Civil (internal) Wars.

Tuesday, May 22nd, was another beautiful blue sky day with open roads ahead. Roney treated her sore and swollen feet to a pedicure before we packed up to leave on the next leg of our Journey. Toni, the masseuse, gave her one of the best massages and treatments Roney ever had, she wanted to stay for more. We started out from Gettysburg southbound on Highway 15 to Frederick, Maryland, to visit two famous Civil War sites on the way to Washington DC and got lost along the way. We had intended to visit both Harpers Ferry and Antietam (where the bloodiest one day battle of the war took place). Well, we got close, but no cigar.

WE CROSSED THE MASON DIXON LINE and about 2.00 pm, gave up the search for the two elusive Civil War sites, stopped for lunch in Frederick and then took Interstate 270 towards Washington. Our FAMOUS sense of timing ensured that we arrived during the height of rush hour, with counter flow lanes against us and then our GPS and helmet radios decided to take the day off. It's such fun riding in heavy rush hour traffic on motorcycles in a strange city when you don't know how to get where you're going and when it's hot. Add in the fact that the upcoming weekend was Memorial Day and, well you get the picture. Anyway, we used our map and our trusty cell phone (we've really come to love those cell phones) to call our B&B and get directions and we made it! We stayed at a nice B&B called the Adams Inn, not far from downtown Washington. After checking in and leaving our bikes, we discovered a wonderful gathering place nearby where students hang out. We would love to make a carbon copy of this in Victoria; it would be a huge success. They serve simple food, very good and nutrious and the drinks vary from smoothies made with fresh fruit to specialty coffees and teas to alcoholic drinks. There were couches and tables and chairs both large and small and, of course, WiFi for the ubiquitous laptops that every student seems to have. Seating about 150, it was a safe place for single people to study or meet up with their friends. We had great fun people watching. We also had the best decaf cappuccino so far on this trip!

On Wednesday, May 23rd, we awoke to another beautiful sunny day on this, our first full day in the Capitol. After breakfast, went downtown on the subway. Once downtown, we joined a hop on hop off tour, which included a fast ride by most of the major sites, including the White House, the Capital Building, the Mall and the various major monuments. After lunch, we went to the Ford Theatre, where President Lincoln was assassinated. Ford Theatre has an excellent museum in the basement dedicated to Lincoln's life. The theatre is pretty much the same as it was at the time of Lincoln's assassination. Even the box seat that he occupied on that fateful evening has been preserved in perpetuity. It was, for us, quite moving to stand at another site of an infamous historical event. Lincoln truly was a great man and certainly one of the Great Presidents of the USA.

We rode a second tour bus line and then had the cheapest dinner we've had on the entire trip, right by the Mall in downtown Washington. Free Beer and 1/2 price pizza in a beautiful outdoor mall, $9.00 for dinner for two. Who said Washington was expensive! Later we went to the Vietnam Veterans Wall, located near the World War ll Memorial. Visiting the Vietnam Veterans Memorial is a very moving experience. It is a simple granite wall, about 300' long, slopping from each end towards the middle. The names of those KIA and MIA are inscribed - the entire wall is covered in names (only names, no personal details). Family members, friends and loved ones come and lay flowers and notes about their sons, daughters, husbands and sweethearts to commemorate their ultimate sacrifices.

We left the Memorial and walked over to visit the Lincoln Memorial and to see the Mall where we came across a Military Group setting up for a Military Tattoo, which was set to start at 6.30 pm. This was a case of being in the right place at the right time. We returned for the Tattoo and it was spectacular. It turns out to be a recruitment event staged by the Military and attended by about 2000 High School kids from all over the states. The Tattoo included a Military Band that played rock music and used talented Military singers performing rock songs. The kids loved it. Soldiers paraded out all the State flags, engaged the kids in various fun activities and had military personnel parade by in uniforms from the Revolutionary War right through the Iraq War. They even had a Fife and Drum band in original Red uniforms and a precision rifle drill team that were absolutely amazing - all for free. We listened to soldiers talk about serving their country and all the aspects of keeping the country free. Towards the end, a soldier in a modern uniform (Roney had her picture taken with him after the event) from Tennessee gave such a moving, inspirational and heart wrenching speech that Colin was ready to sign up right then and there! The soldiers invited everyone down onto the field to visit and take pictures with them and ask any questions that they wanted. We discovered at breakfast the next morning, from parents of two high school children that were guests at the B&B, that many of the kids are enlisted before they start their last couple of years in school and take courses that relate to the field they have chosen in the military. Just a word here on the patriotism of the American people. It was so moving to be at this event when they sang the "Star Spangled Banner" that it was impossible not to be moved to tears. This was probably the most patriotic event we had ever attended; we had to admire the open patriotism that the American people feel for their country. We Canadians are also very patriotic, but we are not quite so open about it. It's too bad, because love of Country is extremely important and we wish we were less reserved when it comes to singing our National Anthem.

Thursday May 24th, and another wonderful day in Washington, DC. We just couldn't go wrong with the weather now with another clear and sunny day ahead. Washington has lots of outdoor eateries and no bugs - literally, we didn't see one insect. We spent the morning making plans for the Memorial Day Weekend, and then headed downtown in the afternoon. First we went to the International Spy Museum where we played some interactive spy games (COOL), then viewed various information and videos of famous spies and lots of the tools of the trade. Then it was on to the Smithsonian Air and Space Museum – wow! Lunar modules, Rockets, IMAX, so much we couldn't take it all in, so we decided to return tomorrow. We decided to add on an extra day, which is the big advantage of having lots of time to play with.

Friday, May 25th and another "Wow" beautiful day in Washington in the high 90's. We set out around noon to visit the Canadian Embassy. Well guess what, they don't let Canadians in, I'm not sure why we pay for it, however it is a beautiful building and is the only Embassy in Washington that the United States donated the land for. After asking for a flag for each of our bikes, we left with two pathetic little paper flags (2" x 3"). Then it was off to visit the Capitol Building. Upon arriving, we learned that all the tickets for the daily tours were gone. A Nice Capitol Policewoman, who was standing nearby when we asked for tickets, said "if you guys are Canadians and have your passports, you can go into the Senate Chamber and watch because it is in session". So off we went to the Security Gate and, with our unbelievably good luck, three of the Capitol Police Officers in the Security Screening Office were very interested in our Motorcycle trip, as they too were bikers. They just couldn't do enough for us. After talking bikes with them and them expressing their amazement that we had ridden so far, they sent us on through to visit the Senate chamber. After getting inside the building, we met up with two young women from Seattle who also wanted to visit the Senate. At one point, we were stopped and told the Senate had recessed until July and we wouldn't be allowed in. Roney immediately went to work and got us through that difficulty by saying we had come all the way from British Columbia, Canada on motorcycles and that this meant so much to us. This got us onto the elevator and on up into the Senate Gallery, where we watched a motion to recess be approved by the only Senator present. So, while we didn't get to see the full Senate in Session, we did get into the Senate Chamber. The two girls from Seattle wanted to hang out with us because they felt we had the power and persuasion to see more than the average American could. As it turned out, we got to see more than what the people on the daily tours see. We will always remember our day at the Capitol Building. After leaving the Senate Chamber, we wandered around the Capitol Building on our own, which seemed kind of unusual, because it is supposed to be a very High Security building. It is a very fascinating building, containing hallways with famous and patriotic sayings and statues of many famous American Citizens.

After seeing as much of the Capitol Building as we wanted, we wandered outside and asked a Capitol Policeman where we could get something nearby to eat and drink. He directed us across the street to the Longworth Building. This turned out to be a Congressional Office Building housing offices of Members of the House of Representatives. We ate in a food court in the building, with Aides and Interns (Monika Lewinsky anyone!). After lunch, we bought a House of Representatives golf shirt and a President of the USA hat, then left to visit two more Smithsonian Museums (of which there are many) and later went to the Pentagon City shopping Mall, where we ate dinner. After dinner, we went back to the Vietnam Veterans Memorial for a Candle light vigil. This being Memorial Day, there were thousands of people there, many arrived on motorcycles. It was quite an experience to be with so many 'baby boomer' veterans, many looking the part of tough biker types, all of whom were there to honour those that did not return from Vietnam. You could hear a pin drop while the vigil lasted, then it was off to the bikes (mostly Harley's), which they fired up, making the ground shake. We wandered around in a market that was set up for the big motorcycle ride called ROLLING THUNDER, set to happen on Sunday. We bought some POW/MIA flags, as we were intending to ride in it, however once we found out more about the scale of the event we decided not to. Rolling Thunder is an Annual Event, staged each Memorial Day Weekend. Biker Veterans from all over the USA converge in DC to ride in Memory of those lost in the Vietnam War. They form up at the Pentagon Parking Lot and then ride en-mass across the Potomac River and up the Mall. Hundreds of thousands ride each year.

Saturday May 26 started out as another hot day, exceeding 95 F. We had thought of going in the Rolling Thunder Ride but the thought of getting into the Pentagon parking lot and then getting out again with 500,000 bikes (yes, that's 500,000) was daunting so we decided to skip the event. We packed up and moved from our B&B into the

Springhill Suites Hotel in Reston, VA, about 40 miles West of DC. Nothing too exciting happened other than getting lost on the way there, and that was because Colin didn't follow the directions of Martha, our trusted GPS. We passed through some gorgeous neighborhoods on the way. That evening, we went out for dinner at a 50's diner called the Silver Diner where they served malts, milk shakes, and huge hamburgers (and I mean huge). After dinner, back at the Springhill Hotel, Roney went out to her bike in the parking to get something and, to her utter horror, the ground moved. Actually, it wasn't the ground, it was worse. A large SNAKE moved under her bike and, needless to say, she screamed (I'm sure she scared the hell out of the snake) and ran up to the room very, very upset. You have to know Roney to understand how traumatic this was. To say she hates snakes is an understatement. Once Colin found out what was wrong, he changed his name to Tarzan (HE HATES SNAKES TOO!) and, with the duty manager, armed with a flashlight, they went out to check Roney's bike (and Colin's as well as under nearby cars and trucks). No snake was found, thank god it was gone, probably more frightened than we were. The staff said they'd never seen any snakes around but why would they say anything else – bad for business! We were told that the heat of the bike might have attracted the snake and that Roney's scream probably got rid of it! We both had trouble sleeping that night. We like to see virtually everything BUT NOT SNAKES.

Apart from the snake incident, Washington, DC was a truly wonderful City to visit. It is the seat of the power for the most powerful nation on earth and it certainly lived up to its billing for us. We did not do justice to the Smithsonian Institute, which has several more museums that we missed. As far as the Mall goes, it gives one an awesome feeling to stand in a place that you have seen many times on TV and, for a short time, to be a part of it. We highly recommend Washington as a must see destination for anyone who loves to travel and experience great cities. It will not disappoint you.

Sunday, May 27th was yet another wonderful hot day. We were told by several locals that this was exceptionally hot weather for May for the east coast. We started out the day with total bedlam in the breakfast area of our Hotel. This was our first truly international breakfast; the guests descended like locusts and ate everything in sight before we arrived. We did finally get a few morsels but couldn't even manage a cup of coffee. With that, it was time to go. We packed up and set off for two communities in Virginia further west of DC, a very affluent part of Virginia. We looked around a place called Middleburg, where the typical vehicles were Aston-Martins, Ford Lotus, with the odd high end Mercedes and BMW. This place oozed money. A local merchant told us they have 12 to 15 Billionaires (that's with a **B**) in an area just west of Middleton called Upperville. That's a lot of moola. After our brief encounter with the 'high flyers', we rode south on Highway 626.   At US Highway 17, also called the Tidewater Trail, we crossed over Interstate 95 (the busiest in the nation) and onto Tappahannouk, VA, where we had lunch and fueled up. We were within a few miles of the birthplace of George Washington, however it was late in the day and his National Monument was closed. We rode on through Glenns, VA, to Highway 238, which took us into Williamsburg. We saw lots of Harleys going home from the Rolling Thunder Ride. We finally arrived in Williamsburg, VA about 8.00 pm and checked into our Timeshare, which is close to the two oldest English settlements in North America, Williamsburg and Jamestown. Our Timeshare Resort, called Powhatan Plantation, is located on 150 acres.

We were very fortunate to arrive during the 400th Anniversary Celebrations for the first permanent British Colony founded at Williamsburg. We continued to have incredible luck at the various places we visited, arriving at just the right time. I like to think it was our precise planning, but maybe it's just Lady Luck at work, smiling on us and our excellent adventure.

Roney standing as close to the White House as we could get.

Colin at the Vietnam Veterans Wall, Washington, DC

Ford's Theatre, Washington, DC

Lincoln's Loge, Ford's Theatre, Washington, DC, site of his assassination

In front of the US Capitol Building, Washington, DC, just before our inside tour

Military Tattoo, Memorial Day Weekend, Washington, DC

Chapter 5 – Williamsburg to Charlottesville, Virginia

Monday, May 28th began as another hot and clear day, over 90 degrees. The first order of business at the new timeshare was to sort out our stuff; boy can things gets messed up and temporarily lost when travelling on two bikes. Despite our best efforts, keeping supplies organized on the bikes became an ongoing challenge. It became apparent that we had to do something about the amount of things we had originally brought with us and the souvenirs and clothes we were acquiring along the way. To say our bikes were overloaded was an understatement. Besides having our hard bags, trunks and suitcases full, we had to load additional items we had acquired on top of our trunks and suitcases, wrapped in plastic garbage bags to protect them from any rain. This had the further disadvantage of raising the centre of gravity on the bikes, which is not something one wants to do on a motorcycle. The time to use FedEx or UPS to send some stuff home had come. Now that we were consistently in hot weather, our foul weather riding gear was at the top of the list of clothes to send home. We got a big box and sorted all of our things into two piles: that which would go on with us and that which we no longer needed and could be shipped home. It was sure nice to be able to get things sorted out and reduce our loads for the next leg of the trip. We packed up quite a large box and shipped it home via the US Postal Service.

The next order of business was to set up house for the week, buy groceries and get organized. Then it was time to go lay by the pool. We were quietly reading beside the pool, enjoying the rays, when we noticed a rather large older looking gentleman. He was wearing a swimsuit, had long white hair, a white beard and mustache and when he laughed his belly "rolled like a bowl full of jelly". (Does this description remind you of a certain fellow that is around in December???). A little girl about four years old walked over to him, stood and looked at him for a few seconds, then asked him if he was Santa Clause. He handled it really well, looking first to the parents of the child for guidance, and, with a nod of assent from them, said he was Santa on a holiday from the North Pole. After watching the interaction with the little girl and this fellow, we introduced ourselves and started chatting to him. He was probably one of the most interesting and funny people we met on this trip. He lives in New York and visits the resort fairly often. He rides down on an old, Heinz 57 Harley that he leaves at his sister's place in Virginia and then takes her car to the resort because, surprise, his Harley leaks oil and the resort frowns on oil stains! He had us in stitches telling us about this bike with its old 'shovelhead engine'. The engine is rigid mounted to the frame, so it shakes, rattles and rolls. Top end is 74 MPH and the bike is loud as hell. Everything vibrates, which gives him double vision. The bike is so loud he has to wear earplugs. His favorite trick when someone cuts him off on the Highway is to pull up beside them, if they're not doing more than 74 mph, turn off the ignition then turn it back on. The bike puts out a flame several feet long and makes a huge backfire, getting the drivers attention, and then he gives the driver a good stare (or scare) then waves to them with a smile. We must have talked to him for an hour. He actually does play Santa Clause and is often approached by children; if fact he was planning on attending a Santa school in Calgary, Alberta, Canada in October. He was just one of the many interesting characters we met on this trip. (We wish we had taken a picture of him). We ended the day writing post cards home. As we were about to go to bed, we were treated to a real big thunderstorm and lots of rain that lasted several hours.

The next morning, Tuesday, May 29, was another warm and sunny day at 95+. It only seems to rain at night here, which made our visit all the more pleasant. When we got up, there was no sign of the rain from the night before. We started the day by going to visit Colonial Williamsburg, the first permanent British Settlement in North America. It was fortunate for us that we arrived on its 400 Anniversary. Williamsburg looks much as it would have in 1607. In addition to the main town site buildings, there is a Governor's Mansion, stables, stores and various other buildings. While we were there, a variety of actors played various roles of events leading up to the Revolutionary War. The costumes were authentic and the whole thing was very well done. During breaks in the action, we wandered the old streets looking into stores, blacksmith's shop, liveries where more costumed people were playing the roles of merchants. The most interesting part of the day was a tour of the rebuilt British Govenor's Mansion from the early 1700's. After it was built, the Second British Governor imported over 850 black powder rifles and handguns and about the same amount of swords which were used to decorate the walls of the entry and main hall. It was his way of intimidating visitors who, of course, had to pass through the entry to see him. We're sure that the amazing amount of weaponry they passed on the way in would have had the desired effect. An elderly lady, 100 years old if she was a day, with a keen sense of humour, gave an interesting tour of the mansion. All the houses in this area were authentic and wonderful to tour. Williamsburg is a must see if you visit the Washington DC area. Washington DC is about a 1 ½ hour drive from Williamsburg.

Wednesday, May 30th   We bought multi-passes on Tuesday for Busch Gardens, Water World and Colonial Williamsburg and today we decided to go to Waterworld and act like kids. We spent the morning and part of the afternoon riding water slides of various kinds and it was a perfect day for it; over 95 degrees and not a cloud in the sky. It was just the perfect kind of day for a water park. We tried every ride in the park and had an absolutely great time, it was not too crowded and we had so much fun it must have been illegal! It was also the day we decided that we had to do something to try and protect ourselves from the intense heat we were experiencing while riding during the hottest part of the year. We knew that from this point on, we would likely be facing many very hot days, not only in the Southeast, Florida and the Gulf Coast, but in the Midwest and Southwest later on during June, July and August. One answer was to start travelling earlier in the day and quit earlier in the day. In addition to that, we decided to purchase two Kevlar vests and two sets of cooling inserts for each vest from Climatech Safety. We had found this company on line and their products looked like the answer to staying cool. The inserts for these vests are filled with a chemical that can be frozen over and over. Once frozen, the inserts are placed in the vest and cool the torso, until they melt. We bought two sets each so that we could wear one until it melted and then replace them with the second set, which we stored in an insulated container. We ordered them from Climatech and had them ship them to us immediately. The balance of the day was spent relaxing by the pool and reading.

Thursday, May 31st. Another hot day, the maximum temperature reached today was 98 F. We went to Busch Gardens in the morning and took two very scary roller coaster rides. Roney surprised me when she said she wanted to ride "The Griffon". This was the latest roller coaster at the park, which had just opened on May 25, 6 days earlier. This ride consists of three rows of seats with 16 seats in each row. The last three people on the end of each row hang out over thin air. The Griffon takes riders up a ramp 205' above the park and then stops with the first row of people over the edge of a straight (yes that's right - straight down) 205' drop. The stop lasts about 5 seconds, then after a loud 'click', it roars straight down 205' feet and into a 180 degree turn, sending you back up and into a half loop so you are upright again, then it repeats the whole thing over and the second time down it goes through water. Roney actually kept her eyes open and had fun on it. Then, big mistake, we went on another ride called 'Alpengiest'. On this one, you spend half the ride upside down and sideways, along with four 360 degree corkscrew turns and it never slows down once.

This ride proved too much for Roney; the poor girl lost her equilibrium, turned several shades of green and had to lie down. Guess as you get older some people can't act like kids on the crazy, fun rides like they used to. Colin had to get her to the First Aid Station so she could lie down and regroup for an hour. She did recover in the Nursing station where she was told that this happens a lot and the heat of the day was also a reason more people where feeling the rush of the rides. After resting and having a cool drink we decided that enough was enough and headed back to our resort. We did a little grocery shopping, some planning for the rest of the week and then relaxed for the balance of the day.

Friday, June 1st. Another hot and humid day with the temperature soaring to 99 degrees. We got up late and, after breakfast, headed out to Norfolk for a harbour tour of the US Naval Base. Norfolk is supposed to be an hour away but took us more than two hours, thanks to a couple wrong turns. It is a very confusing area to drive in and our GPS even got confused. The Interstates here are something to drive on, Interstate 65 is eight lanes and, near Norfolk, it goes through a long tunnel under the Harbour and, Roney, despite her fear of enclosed spaces, came through well for a person with claustrophobia. A really nice lady we met at the Norfolk Visitor Centre gave Roney a big hug when she heard that Roney had ridden through the tunnel on a motorcycle and told her that many locals do not go through that tunnel at the best of times. The tour we took was excellent; we saw much of the US Naval fleet that is based there. Norfolk is now the largest Naval Base in the World. We were fortunate to see many Naval ships (over 40), including three Aircraft Carriers tied alongside each other; the Harry Truman, the Dwight Eisenhower and the Enterprise. These ships are massive - kinda puts our poor little navy to shame. They had just retired one Carrier after 50 years service and are building a new one, which will be called the Gerald Ford. It will take five years to build and, with a lifespan of fifty years, its last captain probably hasn't been born yet. The next name on the list is Bill Clinton, but I guess the Navy is having trouble with that name for a Carrier because of Bill's many escapades- the skipper of our cruise boat said maybe they should name a hospital ship after him, as they have lots of nurses on board! ! The three carriers carry 6,000 personnel each, including flight and maintenance crew, and they serve 18,000 meals a day. Each ship costs several million dollars a day to operate. The might of the US military is truly mind boggling. We rode back to Williamsburg in very heavy traffic, parked for part of the time on a four lane westbound freeway parking lot, creeping forward bit by bit for a half hour until traffic eased up. This kind of stop and go driving on a motorcycle in hot weather is very tiring. We were finally starting to realize that we needed to consider taking rush hours into account when we travel.

Saturday, June 2nd Today started out a little bit cloudy, but it still hit 95 degrees and it was more humid today. We spent part of the day getting ready to move on tomorrow. Roney had a massage while Colin typed up our weekly newsletter and tinkered with the bikes, which were both running well. We've put just over 10,000 kms on them since we left Victoria. The unit we had at this resort was nice. It had a small kitchen and living room, two bathrooms and a loft and the resort was interesting. It was built around an old Plantation called Powhatan, the original Plantation house is still there, having been built in the 1770s. This whole area was interesting because the first permanent British Colonies were established at Williamsburg and Jamestown (about 6 miles from here) in 1607 so there are many historical buildings in the area. We packed up everything we could during the afternoon, in preparation for our departure the following day. We also learned that a Civil War Battle re-enactment was scheduled to take place in one week's time so we decided to alter our plans so we could attend. The Re-enactment was to take place at Mechanicsville, a suburb of the state capital Richmond.   In the meantime, we decided to ride into West Virginia, Kentucky, Tennessee and return via North Carolina before the re-enactment.   This is where our original plan of one week in a timeshare and two weeks in between worked for us.

Sunday, June 3rd We got up to heavy rain, the tail end of Tropical Storm Barry, the first of this Hurricane Season. Winds were gusting to about 40 mph as we left. We put on some of our rain gear before leaving our timeshare so we were ready for anything. We departed

Williamsburg and rode Hwy 199 to Interstate 65 then onto Interstate 295, which goes around Richmond. We took the off ramp into Mechanicsville and went to a Hampton Inn and booked a room for two nights during the Battle Re-enactment. They kindly allowed us to leave some of our stuff, thereby lightening our load on the loop into the west. After finishing at the Hampton Inn, we had lunch at a very entertaining dinner (African Americans having lots of fun on the job) and then carried on west, after an emergency stop at Walmart. We left Richmond on Interstate 64 and the rain picked up as we rode west. We ended the day in Charlottesville Virginia, well short of our goal for the day but the rain was just coming down so hard we were having trouble seeing. Just as it seemed to be raining hard it would rain harder so we called it a day as the road ahead of us heading into the mountains was really foggy. Our inner clothes and feet were wet and we were starting to get pretty cold and grouchy. We checked into a hotel, got out of our wet clothes and dried out.

British Govenor's Mansion, Williamsburg, Virginia

CHAPTER 6 – WEST VIRGINIA, KENTUCKY, TENNESSEE, NORTH CAROLINA & VIRGINIA

Monday, June 4th   Monday dawned to nice weather, the previous days storm was gone. Just to make sure it stayed nice, we put on all our rain gear and headed west on Interstate 64. About 30 miles west of Charlottesville, we turned south onto what is one of the prettiest roads in the USA - the Blue Ridge Parkway. After fueling up at Afton, Virginia, we began our ride down the two lane highway that runs along a ridge of the Appellation Mountains (on a range know as the Blue Mountains). This road is filled with spectacular vistas, wonderful bends and was just a pleasure to ride. The Parkway ran for 90 miles and we met very few vehicles, other than other motorcycles. Our two way radios worked well for once so we were able to share in all the great sites we were seeing with each other. At the end of the Parkway, we turned onto an awesome road that had lots of twists and turns (just what we motorcyclists love) and hooked up with Interstate 64 at Lexington, Va. We rode onto Covington, VA, where we fueled up and then continued on across the West Virginia border, past White Sulphur Springs and into Lewisville, West Virginia, just as rain started to fall. Had a great visit with some truckers over dinner, who were able to give us some good advice for the following day. Riding into West Virginia brought to mind John Denver's song "Country Roads, Take Me Home". The countryside was very pretty and the roads were definitely like the Country Roads John Denver had in mind. We had just gotten to the hotel in Lewisburg and parked our bikes under a sheltered area in front of the hotel as the skies really opened up (we were not even registered yet)! We were treated to a thunder and lightning storm most of the evening while staying in the least expensive accommodation so far, the Brier Inn. Lewisville was a very quiet community and we had a great night's sleep that night.

On Tuesday, June 5th we left Lewisville, WVa at 9.30 under partly cloudy skies but no rain. We rode west on Interstate 64 to Crab Orchard, then headed west on Highway 54 through Hotchkiss to Mayben, where we turned onto Highway 97, passing through Newfound, and Baileyville, WVa and on into Hanover. From Hanover we took Hwy 52 to Williamson, where we fueled up and had a snack (Williamson is on the West Virginia, Kentucky border). We took Highway 119 to Pikeville, Kentucky and checked into a hotel for the night. We even rode through Canada, West Virginia that day. The riding absolutely fantastic, the County and rural roads had little or no traffic, lots of pretty scenery, plenty of twists and turns and friendly people. The roads were dry and the weather stayed nice all day. That same day, hailstones as big as 1" in diameter were falling to the north of us, but missed us completely. We passed through a couple of small West Virginia Towns that appeared to have fallen on hard times. West Virginia still relies to some extent on coal mining, however many of those towns now appear all but dead. People there were nice, the countryside is pretty, but the towns themselves were very rundown. Pikeville, Kentucky is relatively small, with a population about 6000, but it is also famous, or should we say, infamous.

The Hatfield/ McCoy Feud took place near Pikeville during the late 1800s along the Tug Fork River. We arrived in Pikeville purely by chance and were pleasantly surprised that it was a great point of interest. Legend has it that a Roseanna McCoy had an affair with Johnse Hatfield, Roseanna became pregnant and Johnse left her to marry his cousin Ellison Hatfield in 1881. Another legend says that the famous feud began in 1882 when Ellison Hatfield was murdered by Tolbert, Pharmer and Bud McCoy. The McCoy brothers were later murdered in revenge by members of the Hatfield family. Descendants of the families now say that the feud was simply the result of disputes over land lines and water rights. The Tug Fork, a tributary of the Big Sandy River, divided the property of the two families, the Hatfield's property being on the West Virginia side of the Tug Fork, while the Mc Coy's property was on the Kentucky side. Both families were amongst the first settlers in the Tug Valley and both families were very involved in making moonshine. During the Civil War, the Hatfield's supported and served in the Union Army while the McCoy's supported and served the Confederacy. Just these simple facts are enough for us to understand how this famous family feud was possible. In 1891, the two warring families finally agreed to a truce, ending the feud between them. Some say, the feud lives on in the hearts and minds of some of their family members today. A story we heard locally was that the two families reunited at a 'Hillbilly Fair' that takes place annually in Pikeville, where they poke fun at their ancestors and each other.

Now here's an interesting thing that happened Tuesday evening. People have been incredibly friendly everywhere we've been. For instance, the owner of the hotel we stayed in let Colin use the computer behind the reception counter to work on our newsletter, (got to love that). Colin then called Phil at the Motorcycle Accessory Centre in Calgary to try and obtain new highway bars for Roney's bike, which we couldn't find at any of the bike shops we'd visited (another lesson to be learned that you cannot always get "after market" parts for brand new bikes). When Phil found out that we were riding in southern Kentucky, he said, you've got to go ride 'The Dragon' in Tennessee. We said, "What's the Dragon?" he said, "Only the most awesome motorcycle highway in North America located just south of Knoxville by the Great Smokey Mountain National Park". He said he'd ridden it once at night and hadn't been able to buy a tee-shirt and asked if we would get him one if we decided to do it. Here we are in Kentucky and we hadn't heard of it and we find out about it from a friend in Calgary. So, rather than go to horse country in the Lexington area of Kentucky (home of the Kentucky Derby), **no contest**, we decided to go ride the Dragon! We also heard of the Biltmore Estate, but more about that later.

Wednesday, June 6th We left Pikeville early in thick fog (ok, now the only weather condition we have not travelled in is tornados and hurricanes) which cleared up about an hour after we left Pikeville. We headed south for Knoxville, Tennessee via Highway 119 to the Tennessee State Line, then onto Highway 23 to Interstate 81 which we took into Knoxville, arriving there rather speedily at noon. After lunch, we headed west on Interstate 40 looking for the Dragon and, of course, we got lost. We finally found Alcoa, TN, fueled up and headed out onto 'the Dragon', which is located just south of Marysville, at about 2 pm.   Now, about the Dragon. Its official name is US Highway 129 but it's widely known as 'the "Tail of the Dragon" at Deal's Gap. The 'Dragon' is considered by many north American bikers to be the #1 motorcycle and sports car road on the Continent, perhaps in the World. It even has its own website and specialty shops at both ends selling every kind of souvenir from tee shirts, mugs, hats, patches, decals, etc. THIS HIGHWAY CONSISTS OF **TWO LANES WITH 318 TIGHT CURVES IN 11 MILES.** The road is very, very narrow and a real challenge for the experienced rider. Believe us, it is as challenging to ride as any road we have ever seen and now we can say we rode it. Colin even went in the ditch on one corner, no injuries to him or the bike, just to his pride! The ride was particularly challenging for us as we were fully loaded with all of our stuff, whereas most bikers ride it with as little on their bikes as possible. It was the most fun and challenging of any road we have ever ridden. And, of course, we bought the tee shirts, including one for Phil in Calgary. We shopped at a biker's store at the south end of the Dragon's Tail, where a hundred or so bikes were stopped, shopped and then moved on.   The Dragon's Tail is challenging for more than just its curves. It's about the other bikers and sports cars riding it at the same time. It's not a long ride from Atlanta, so every day lots of bikers come up and ride it both ways. The Crotch Rockets would come around inside corners with one knee almost on the pavement and on the wrong side (our side) of the road.

So, not only did we have to negotiate our own bikes around these challenging bends but we had to keep a sharp eye out and be prepared to take evasive action at every corner to avoid other bikers oncoming or passing us on the left or right! Now we can say we've done it and never need to do it again. We'll never forget US Highway 129. Besides being the most challenging road in North America, it also has the dubious distinction of claiming many lives. Semis are specifically prohibited from using it. Checked out the Website for photos of various semi mishaps from the past (see Reference Section for Web address).

After our encounter with The Dragon's Tale at Deals Gap, we rode on to Topton, North Carolina on Highway 129, then turned east onto Highway 74 and rode into Waynesville, NC. We picked up new highway bar for the Kawasaki at Waynesville Cycle Centre, which our friend Phil in Calgary had arranged for, installed it and headed out again eastbound on Interstate 40 to Asheville, North Carolina. We had almost circumnavigated the Great Smokey Mountains National Park during our ride today and it was very evident how the Park acquired its name. These Mountains appear quite smokey from the west and south.

Ashville, NC, is the home of Biltmore Estate, which we mentioned earlier. The Biltmore Estate was built between 1888 - 1895 by one George Vanderbilt, a grandson of the famous Cornelius Vanderbilt who created a vast empire in the nineteenth century. Cornelius began as a worker on Staten Island ferries in New York. He eventually bought steamships and eventually railroads. By the time he passed away in 1877, he had amassed a fortune estimated at $100 Million (a vast sum in 1877). Cornelius was ruthless in business and trusted only one of his sons with the vast majority of his business assets; William Henry Vanderbilt. William received $100 Million and by the time of his death in 1885, he had increased his worth to $194 Million (in eight years!). George Vanderbilt, who built the Biltmore Estate, inherited $1 million dollars from his grandfather, Cornelius, when he died in 1877, then an additional $1 million on his 21st birthday from his father. When his father died in 1885, he received another $5 million as well as the income on a trust account of $5 million. George was not a businessman like his father and grandfather; rather he sought out intellectual pursuits. He loved North Carolina and had the largest private residence in North America constructed there consisting of 175,000 sq. ft. with 255 rooms (much larger than Hearst Castle in California) built to look like a French Chateau. There, he took up the life of a country gentleman, however the cost to operate Biltmore eventually outstripped his financial resources and he had to dip into his capitol. Despite that, it has remained in the family and is still operated by Vanderbilt descendants as a tourist attraction. We decided to treat ourselves to a night at the Biltmore Inn, which is on the estate grounds. It is a luxury 6 Star hotel and was it gorgeous or what! We didn't do much that evening, after all, we had ridden for 10 hours with only a couple of breaks, so we ate in the room and crashed (people DRESS for dinner in the dining room and we only had blue jeans). We were treated exceptionally well by the doorman and staff. It never ceases to amaze us just how many people ride, have ridden or want to ride a motorcycle at some time. We were given preferential treatment, partly because we were on motorcycles and all the way from British Columbia, Canada but also because we always tried our best to be nice to everyone as well. After all, we were Canadian and Biker Ambassadors! The doorman arranged for us to park our bikes in a private lot (for Staff Only) and Security kept an eye on them overnight. Staying at this hotel was one of many special highlights on this, our trip of a lifetime.

Thursday, June 7th   Another beautiful and hot day in the high 90's. We woke up late and, dressed in fresh jeans, went for breakfast in the fabulous dining room at the Biltmore Inn (yes, you can dress casually for breakfast). After breakfast, we packed and then took a tour of the fabulous Biltmore Estate. This estate was created by George Washington Vanderbilt, after he holidayed in Ashville North Carolina in the late 1800s. He liked it so much he bought 125,000 acres and set about building the largest home imaginable. The house is still in the same condition as it was then. The design included 65 fireplaces, it was completely wired for electricity (keep in mind it was built between 1889 and 1895) and it was built with fireproof walls sectioning the house into 6 fireproof zones, so that in the event of a fire, no more than

1 section could burn. It had its own telephone system and a system to communicate with servants and other staff. The tour of the house took about 1 hour and it was breathtaking. Roney has been through Hearst Castle and she thinks the stables at Biltmore might be larger than Hearst Castle. This was like watching the ultimate lifestyles of the rich and famous from the 1800s. If you ever find yourselves visiting North Carolina, this is a MUST SEE. After completing our tour, we went back to the hotel and, while loading up the bikes, Roney met a man from Richmond, who rides a BMW, and he gave us all sorts of information on Richmond, which was where we were going in a couple of days. He told us about the 4 corners club (riders doing what we're doing) and even invited us to a bike meet on the weekend in Richmond.

We departed just after lunch, rode out onto Interstate 40 and off to High Point, NC, the centre of furniture manufacturing in the US. After a rather rapid ride of 2 1/2 hours we arrived in the High Point area without finding High Point. This was a rather nerve racking ride as Interstate 40 is heavily used by trucks. At times we had trucks in front, behind and on both sides. This is not an Interstate to daydream on.

We stopped at a gas station, fueled up and had a conversation with a young couple, who directed us to where we needed to go. The young woman was a teacher and when she found out we were from Canada, said "Oh Wow, I've never met a Canadian before"! How cool is that? We did find High Point, where we checked into a hotel. At dinner, we met a wonderful server named Tammera, who was a lot of fun. She made Roney a float and Colin a milkshake, even though they weren't on the menu (she said I make them for my kids so I'll just see what I can find in the kitchen and be right back!) Now is that service or what? After chatting with her for some time we felt comfortable enough to ask her how much servers made in North Carolina and were shocked at how low the wages were (under $4.00 per hour) and left her a good tip when we were finished. Once again, we're meeting the greatest people on this trip - it just keeps getting better and better. High Point is definitely a furniture city - everywhere there are furniture stores and manufacturers, however most do not admit the public. They have a huge conference hall where manufacturers showcase their wares to retailers. They claim to be 'the furniture capital of the world'.

Friday, June 8th, another very, very hot day, into the high 90s by midafternoon. We set out about 9.30 am intending to go to an area of the City of High Point where furniture is sold to the Public - well, we missed it and ended up in Greensboro, then went north on Highway 29, through Danville, Chatham and Rustburg into Appomattox, Virginia. We had decided the night before to visit Appomattox Courthouse, the site where Confederate General Robert E Lee surrendered to Union General Ulysses Grant on April 9th, 1865, which occurred the same week that Lincoln was shot by John Wilkes Booth. The US National Park Service operates it as a National Historic Site. It was quite a feeling to stand in the original McLean home and look at the actual table in the parlor of the McLean House where General Lee signed the surrender for the Army of North Virginia, which essentially ended the Civil War and reunited the country. The son of the owner of the plantation was allegedly the first casualty of the war. He enlisted for the south and died two months after he enlisted of disease and never saw battle. Many of the young farm boys did not have immunity to the diseases that the "city boys" had, consequently many died of diseases rather than in battle. Nearby was a gravesite with 17 graves, 16 were Confederate soldiers and 1 Union soldier. The estimated number of deaths during the 4 years of the civil war was 630,000, an astounding figure!

The area around Appomattox is very pretty, rolling hills, forested with open meadows. We continued on into Richmond, Virginia on Highway 24 to Highway 60 and, while trying to find our hotel, went through a very established neighborhood that would put our Uplands to shame. Beautiful antebellum and Victorian homes set on quiet streets with large trees on both sides meeting overhead. Wow, just fantastic!

Saturday, June 9th Another very beautiful, but very hot day in the high nineties. After breakfast, we headed off to the Civil War reenactment at Mechanicsville, something that we were really looking forward to. This re-enactment is held on a large piece of private property east of Richmond and reenacts the Battle of Mechanicsville that occurred there in June 1862, when the Union Army attempted to surround Richmond (the capital of the Confederacy) but failed. Numerous vendors were set up to sell food and various wares, most of which related to the Civil War in one way or another. The vendors were a wonderful group of people, most were very interested in our trip. We roamed around looking at what they had to offer, had lunch and then went to meet the 'Generals'. The Generals are, in real life, computer programmers, construction workers, administrators, etc. All of the Generals were Confederate Officers (remember, Virginia was in the South). The most important Generals were there - Lee, Stonewall Jackson, Longstreet, Stuart, etc and the portrayers looked amazingly like the real characters. Before the reenactment began, there was a demonstration of 1860's artillery. The Generals then spoke about 'their characters' role in the War and how they viewed the war as an aggression by the North. Each said the underlying cause was not slavery, but taxation without representation. Apparently 52% of the US Budget came from the South before the War and only 25% of the US budget was spent in the South. Sounds a bit like Western Canada! Before the Generals left to go to the battlefield, we approached them and took each other's photos with them. General Stuart looked at Roney and said "Are you Northern Sympathizers?" She said "No" and he said "Why are you wearing a Yankee hat". Roney had put a New York Yankees ball cap on before leaving the hotel to protect her head from the intense heat without thinking of the reenactment. Of course, all of this was done in jest and we all got a chuckle out of it, but before we went to the viewing area to watch the reenactment, we went to one of the vendors and bought Roney a Confederate Hat. The reenactment included Cavalry charges, infantry movements and Artillery - the noise was impressive - the 'battle' lasted for about 1 1/2 hours and was most entertaining. After a brief rest, they went at it again. None of the Northern Officers were introduced and, of course, the Union troops eventually lost the battle.

Also present was a replica of the "Hunley" first Confederate Submarine used in the Civil War. The submarine was about 40' long and was operated by a number of men who turned a crankshaft that turned a propeller. A small tube could be sent up to the surface to take in fresh air and a candle was lit so that the crew would know when their oxygen supply was running out. They used a crude periscope to see where they were going and the 'sub' was fitted with a long metal shaft on the bow onto which a explosive charge was affixed with a barbed hook. If everything went right, the sub could approach a moored ship at night, ram the charge into the ships wooden hull and then back away by reversing the prop. A line attached to the charge, which was now impaled in the hull, was also attached to the submarine. As the sub backed away, the line would go tight and arm the charge. This was intended to give the sub crew time to escape. At least one northern ship was sunk in this manner. The submarine reminded us of a metal coffin, appropriately black in color.

We really enjoyed the people we had met in the South; they can't do enough for visitors, particularly to those of us on motorcycles. We made some new friends there and left, rather exhausted, for a rest and to spend some time in the SHADE. We spent the evening at the hotel getting ready to move onto the Outer Banks.

Sunday, June 10th The temperature dropped somewhat which made for better riding conditions. 86 degrees was so nice for a change. We left Richmond on Interstate 64 then 264 heading for Virginia Beach, where we strolled down to the beautiful beach and along 'the strip'. There were thousands of people walking around, shopping, lying on the beach and just enjoying the day. What a place, especially if you are between 15 and 25 (or with Roney). After a nice lunch by the beach, we headed back to our bikes. We left Virginia Beach and headed for Highway 168 at Chesapeake, then headed south across the state line into North Carolina. Highway 168 winds along the western shore of the Inland Coastal Waterway, the protected body of water between the Outer Banks and the Continental shore. There were many beautiful vistas along this stretch of coastline, including water and the outer islands. We linked up with Highway 158 at Barco, North Carolina and continued south along a peninsula to Point Harbor, where we took the bridge across Currituck Sound onto the Outer Banks. Shortly thereafter, we discovered that we were at Kitty Hawk near Kill Devil Hills, NC, the place where the Wright Brothers made their first flight in 1903. There is a great monument to their achievement and an impressive display of their aircraft. The area has changed little since the Wright Brothers worked and flew their heavier than air machine there for the first time on December 17, 1903. The site is now a National Historic Site operated by the National Park Service.

We continued south from Kill Devil Hills through Nags Head on Highway 158 on the outer Banks, then took NC Highway 12 (Cape Hatteras National Park Road) through Cape Hatteras National Seashore to the town of Ocracoke. It was a wonderful ride between Kitty Hawk and Ocracoke, riding the thin strip of land between the Atlantic Ocean and the Inland Waterway; it was almost like riding on water. We were fortunate that the winds were light, the sky was clear and the traffic was even lighter. The number # 1 beach in the World award for 2006 was awarded to the Outer Banks, which we were able to see. Luckily, we checked in at a Visitors Centre because we had to book both a place to stay and a 2 hour and 15 minute ferry ride the next day. It was a long day but worth it. If we had been there any other day of the week we would have been able to see the longest running outdoor play in America. It was about the first people to settle in this area.

The Outer Banks are fairly flat in this area and largely composed of sand. Many of the homes are built on stilts and many of them are summer/weekend homes. We stayed in the Ocracoke Island Inn, a lovely old Inn, dating back to the early 1800s and had a nice evening walking around the wharfs looking at the Deep Sea Fish Boats.

*Roney admiring the view from the Shenandoah Parkway,
western Virginia*

*Roney in front of the Biltmore Estate, Ashville, North Carolina,
home of the Vanderbilt's*

*The MacLean House, Appomattox National Historic Site, Virginia,
Site where General Robert E. Lee surrendered to General Ulysses Grant
on April 9, 1865s*

*Confederate officers at Mechanicsville Battle reenactment. General
Robert E. Lee on the left and General "Stonewall Jackson" on the right.*

Battle reenactment at Mechanicsville, Virginia (outside Richmond)

Three "flat tops" at Norfolk Naval Station, Norfolk, Virginia.

Colin "flying" at Kitty Hawk National Historic Site, Kitty Hawk, North Carolina

One of the many wonderful mansions in Richmond, Virginia,

CHAPTER 7 – CAPE HATTERAS, NC TO ST AUGUSTINE, FL

Monday, June 11th Colin's Birthday - yes, he's a dreaded Gemini! This was the first cool morning we'd had in some time and it was welcome. We were up early for the departure of the Carolina Ferry from the Cape Hatteras Islands to Cedar Island, a 2 hour trip. We watched people feeding the gulls as we crossed and just relaxed on the pleasant crossing. We disembarked the ferry onto Highway 12 and continued south until we hooked up with US Highway 70 and then onto Highway 24 and later onto Highway 17 so that we could continue hugging the coast. At Myrtle Beach, a very popular Beach community about two thirds of the way to Charleston, we decided to take the waterfront drive (Ocean Boulevard) which took us down the strip of Myrtle Beach. As the day progressed the temperature rose drastically. This drive was about 20 miles long and it was wall to wall traffic. It took us over 2 hours to clear Myrtle Beach and get going again. The exhaust from the cars and trucks was almost unbearable along with the heat. We could see the heat waves off the asphalt it was so hot. We arrived in Charleston after dark, missed a turn and ended up in a part of town that wasn't very historic and didn't seem like a good area to be in. In fact, we were getting some pretty hostile looks from the local youths so we quickly exited, got back on the Interstate and, this time, made our way to our B&B, which we had booked on line before we left Victoria and which turned out to be the worst accommodations we had had so far. The elderly lady that ran it was a nice Southern Lady but the room was small, the bed was hard and there no hot water for showers or to soak our weary bones. Overall, we had a great ride today, saw some fantastic scenery and oceanscapes and met more nice people. We had a lovely dinner out to celebrate Colin's birthday. It was one of Colin's better birthdays, celebrated in a beautiful southern city in the company of a beautiful woman.

Tuesday, June 12th. The weather today was overcast and cooler, in the mid-eighties. We took in the Open Market in Charleston which, prior to the Civil War, was a slave market; we wandered through it and bought a few things. Then we set off to explore the downtown area on foot. Downtown, we reserved a room for the following day, knowing that sleep would probably elude us again tonight in the HARD BED. Later, we went for dinner and then went for a stroll through an area of historic southern homes. WOW - they were absolutely beautiful. True Southern Antebellum homes. We wandered around for several hours on foot looking at them and taking photos until well after dark, then had to find our way back to the B&B and let the nice little old lady know we were moving the next day. Charleston is such a gentile, charming, old wealthy city. It oozes Southern Charm, refinement, money, manners, upper-class and real southern hospitality. Colin was particularly impressed with the lovely homes on the shore overlooking the bay where Fort Sumter is located. Even our hostess spoke in such refined terms, it made us smile. For example, she referred to the new owner of our Hudson's Bay Company in Canada as the "rear end of a mule" instead of an ass. She said he inherited his money and had no class! She said he buys lots of companies but doesn't know anything about running them, just buys them. That evening we ate at Diana's Cafe Cafe in downtown Charleston (that's not a typo). We were very impressed with the food, service and prices in the Deep South, which were very reasonable. We had an excellent meal for two for under $40.00 – thoroughly enjoyed it. We finished our evening off by returning to the B&B and packing up for the move to the King Charles Inn.

Wednesday, June 13 another overcast day. We loaded our bikes after breakfast and moved our stuff to a nice Best Western Hotel right downtown. Then we went to the other side of the harbour, where the US Navy has the decommissioned USS Yorktown aircraft carrier at Patriots Point. We bought some naval hats and then went for a harbour tour, which included a visit to Fort Sumter. The Confederacy fired the first shots of the Civil War from Charleston at Fort Sumter on April 12, 1861, probably because it was handy and South Carolina was the first state to succeed from the Union. We were accumulating a lot of Civil War knowledge as the trip progressed. The commentator on our Harbour tour boat was just announcing over the PA that the first shot of the Civil War was fired on Fort Sumter when a very loud crack and an explosion was heard as a bolt of lightning struck a tall harbor bridge just behind our boat. A threatening storm with a dark sky had crept up on us while we were enroute to Fort Sumter and some passengers were a little nervous. Well the storm hit with a vengeance and the storm continued most of the day with major rain, hail, and naturally our bikes were parked in an outdoor lot. Unfortunately for us, we left our helmets turned upright and, yes, that means that we got very wet heads when we put them on to go back to our hotel after the harbour tour (lesson learned the hard way, always put the helmets on the bike properly). We thoroughly enjoyed our visit to Fort Sumter, where we viewed the huge cannons used during the start of the Civil War, the battlements and accommodations. After returning to shore (and our wet helmets) we recrossed the river to downtown and took our bikes back to the Hotel. Then we took off walking with our umbrellas and cruised the market again, (buying a lovely table cloth and napkins), then went for dinner and got repacked to head onward to Savannah, Georgia the next day. Dinner that evening was at "Sticky Fingers", a southern restaurant chain with absolutely delicious 'finger sticking' ribs. We went home full and content after dinner and slept like logs.

Thursday, June 14, we got up to an overcast morning, but no rain. After the great sleep in our new hotel, we finished packing up the bikes, had breakfast and set out for Savannah, Georgia. We left Charleston on Highway 17 and hooked up with Interstate 95 at Pocotalgo, then rode Interstate 95 to Hardeeville from where we took Highway 17 into Savannah, Georgia. We had a nice ride and enjoyed the scenery of the old South, the only problem we encountered was with our two way radios on the Interstate, again they decided not to work. We missed going to a beautiful plantation on the way but we knew there would be many more of them. This time, Martha (our GPS) guided us right to the East Bay Inn in beautiful Savannah, right in the heart of old town. We checked into a beautiful and romantic room. We had prebooked the East Bay Inn before we left home and were not disappointed. After bussing our stuff up to our room, we set out on a walk of the old historic waterfront. Savannah is another 'old southern city' with wonderful friendly and helpful people. The Inn had a happy hour just after we arrived and two couples were very intrigued with our trip. They were from Florida and both suggested we visit St. Augustine, which neither of us had heard of before. Once again, we found out more information about interesting places to visit along the way than we ever could have on line or from the tourist information packages we ordered before leaving home. We had dinner at Riverfront Seafood, where Roney's son Sean had taken her when she was there with him a few years before. After dinner we walked around the waterfront where Sean's yacht had been docked and we looked at the old buildings that were used to store and ship cotton overseas in the 1800's. The houses were just as beautiful as some that we saw in Charleston, but were in need of some TLC. Spanish moss hanging from tress branches was very predominant here and it looked quite lacy and spooky at night. Spanish moss although it looks lovely, is full of bugs so you don't want to sit under it. We went on a ghost tour which we found very interesting.

Friday, June 15th Another mixed weather day, partly overcast but still hot and humid and in the mid-eighties. We took Roney's bike into a Kawasaki dealer for service and met the neatest bunch of guys at Beasley Kawasaki Polaris. The mechanic went over Roney's bike while she was in the mechanic's shop and gave her several tips. She decided he was the best mechanic she's ever met because he didn't talk down to her **(all you bike shop guys – remember lots of women ride bikes and they spend plenty on them too).** Roney checked out a fully loaded Kawasaki Vulcan 1500 cc motorcycle and 'drooled'. We then rode "two up" on Colin's bike back into town, had lunch and then decided to go to a 'Fifties Musical' that evening. After buying tickets, we went back and picked up Roney's bike and then it was back downtown to shop (Roney knows how to do many things well, but she got a PHD in shopping). She knows how to shop for good prices and nice things to remember trips by.

While downtown, we visited the park where Tom Hanks played the part of Forrest Gump, for which he won an Academy Award for Best Actor. It was neat to be able to sit on the same park bench where he spoke to various people and said the famous words "And that's all I have to say about that". Some googling indicated that Forrest Gump was fictional and that the character in the film was based on the Vietnam exploits of a US soldier who won the Congressional Medal of Honour for extreme heroism in 1967 and was wounded in the "buttocks". Either way, we did visit the site where that portion of the film was shot. The restaurant chain Bubba Gump Shrimp Company, portrayed in the movie, is certainly real and we enjoyed several meals at their restaurants during the course of our travels.

After dinner, we had to hurry to get to the theatre on time because the weather turned sour. We had one of those tropical rain and hail storms which lasted a couple of hours, so we only managed a coffee and a pastry for dinner. The musical was great with a cast of about 14 musicians and dancers who did all the great hits of the 50's; from Elvis, the Everly Bros, the Big Bopper, Patty Page, Fats Domino, etc. It was highly entertaining and there was a large group of 'silver tips' sitting opposite us who were in seventh heaven. Out of the all songs that they sang Roney knew all but one. Later we went back to the Inn and made reservations for St. Augustine, using information from other guests we met at the Inn.

Saturday, June 16th   The weather was nice with clear skies and no sign of rain in the morning. We packed up, checked out and, once again, we took the 'scenic route' to get to Interstate 95, which added an extra 20 miles. We had a great run down Interstate 95 to Jacksonville, FL. By now, we were becoming quite comfortable riding on this massive and extremely busy Interstate, weaving in and out like old pros. Interstates 95 and 40 (east of Asheville, North Carolina) were the two busiest freeways we rode on during the entire trip. We stopped in Jacksonville, Florida for lunch and to try and pick up a Civil War bullet for Roney from a vendor we had met at the Civil War Reenactment in Richmond who had promised her a Civil War bullet if we stopped in Jacksonville. Well, we stopped and he was out, so much for the Civil War bullet. We had lunch and then continued onto US Highway 1 just south of Jacksonville and rode on into St. Augustine, arriving around 4.00 pm. It was extremely hot by this time; we just had a plunge into the pool and then retreated to the air conditioned room at our hotel. As you can appreciate, we don't have laundry facilities on the bikes and we were almost at the point of having to beat our clothes to death so we could put them on, so it turned out to be a laundry day. Clean underwear never felt so good! Thanks to a close by restaurant, we did takeout that evening.

Sunday, June 17th Fathers Day, we awoke to a beautiful day, not a cloud in the sky with the temperatures in the high 90's and 98% humidity. We had breakfast in downtown St Augustine and then set out to explore (shop) the town. Roney was in her glory, we found a few interesting things to buy and lots of great things to look at. Briefly, St. Augustine is the oldest **European** settlement in North America. It was settled by the Spanish starting in 1565. They built a very strong fortress and remained there well into the 1700's. It has a Spanish Quarter where some of the buildings date back to the 1600's, all of which now have shops in them. We toured the old Spanish Fortress, which is a National Monument administered by the National Park Service. We had a great afternoon wandering around and then went to the Library to use a computer and complete our Weekly Newsletter. We frequently used local libraries to bring our weekly newsletters up to date and to send them. Virtually every library we visited provided 'free' computer access to the general public, which was great, because we really didn't need to be packing a laptop with us. We usually offered a small donation to each library, which was gratefully accepted. We really appreciated the friendly service we received at the many libraries where we used public computers to access the internet. We did find that almost every hotel we stayed in during our 2007 trip offered Wifi, so a small laptop would have been nice to have, provided we could have kept it clean and dry.

Colin at Fort Sumter National Historic Site, Charleston, South Carolina.

Performers on the Waterfront in charming Savannah, Georgia

Square in Savannah used in the filming of "Forest Gump".

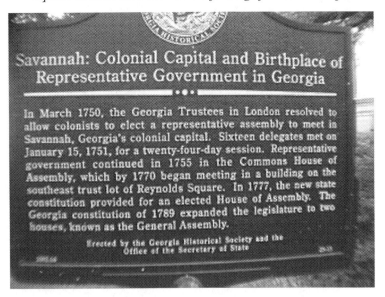

Savannah: Colonial Capital and Birthplace of Representative Government in Georgia

In March 1750, the Georgia Trustees in London resolved to allow colonists to elect a representative assembly to meet in Savannah, Georgia's colonial capital. Sixteen delegates met on January 15, 1751, for a twenty-four-day session. Representative government continued in 1755 in the Commons House of Assembly, which by 1770 began meeting in a building on the southeast trust lot of Reynolds Square. In 1777, the new state constitution provided for an elected House of Assembly. The Georgia constitution of 1789 expanded the legislature to two houses, known as the General Assembly.

Erected by the Georgia Historical Society and the Office of the Secretary of State

Historical Interest Sign in Savannah, Georgia

Roney taking a time out in St. Augustine, Florida

Chapter 8 – St. Augustine, FL to Delray Beach, FL

Monday, June 18th. Today we woke up to another blistering hot day; by 8.00 am it was around 85 and rising without a cloud in the sky. This turned out to be the hottest day we have encountered so far as the temperature reached over 105 degrees!! This was tooooo hot. We had given our cooling vest inserts to the Hotel the previous evening and they put them in a freezer overnight. After packing the bikes, we put on our vests (front, side and rear) with the frozen coolant inserts. This really helped.

We saddled up our iron steeds (well it sounds better than "put our stuff on our bikes") and set out south from St. Augustine about 9.30 am. After talking to some local folks as well as some guests at the hotel in Savannah, we decided to take the scenic route, Highway A1A, which hugs the coast and, at times, goes out onto the outer islands that form part of the 'Intercoastal Waterway'. For our landlubber friends, the Intercoastal waterway is a partially man made (dredged) and partly natural channel that runs up the east coast of the USA from Florida, more or less unbroken, to New England. It allows vessels to go up and down much of the coast without going into the open Atlantic waters. We have nothing like this on the west coast, with the exception of Vancouver Island and the Inside passage north of Vancouver Island.

The ride along A1A today was awesome. The colour of the ocean is just like the Caribbean Sea, kind of a green blue and there were virtually no swells. The surrounding countryside was fairly low lying and flat, covered with plants and areas that looked like prime alligator habitat, although we hadn't seen any Gators yet. Also, many of the oceanfront homes were spectacular. Roney took lots of photos. We rode on A1A into Daytona Beach, home of the famous Daytona Speedway and the Daytona 500. Daytona is also home to Daytona Bike week each year in March, which is an even bigger event than Sturgis Bike Week in South Dakota. They get as many as 600,000 bikes of all kinds converging here from all over the country. Of course we had to get the T-shirts so we went to the famous Speedway and visited the gift shops. Colin had to have a look at the famous track with its 30 degree banked curves and it certainly is very impressive. We bought a few things then went looking for a motorcycle Toy shop and did we strike gold! Daytona has a Bikers Mall, yes a mall with several very large big box biker's stores that sell almost everything for motorcycles including motorcycles. We were very good, we just looked and didn't buy anything, but oh it was tempting.

We have finally developed the idea of starting out earlier in the day to avoid the intense heat but today, we wanted to stop in Daytona and it was getting on, so we got onto Interstate 95 to make up some time. After and hour and a half on I 95 going like hell, we arrived in Titusville, the nearest city to the Kennedy Space Centre, where we checked into the "Best Western Space Shuttle Hotel" and jumped into the swimming pool to cool off. People we met in the pool told us of an awesome buffet restaurant close by so we went there for dinner. We just bummed around that evening and Colin stuck another decal on his windshield (which he has been collecting along the way). We also decided to do a slight side trip to the Bahamas for 2 days the following week and booked it online as well as a cheap flight from Spirit Air, flying out of Fort Lauderdale. There's nothing quite like taking a holiday from a holiday!

We were watching the weather to the west, particularly for Texas as it was on our list of states to visit and at that time they were having a lot of heavy rain and floods. It was reported on the weather channel that 2" of rain fell in one hour near San Antonio where several people lost their lives because of flash floods. Not a safe place to ride motorcycles, so we were monitoring the weather daily.

Tuesday, June 19 Today started out to be another hot one, with some cloud cover, even so, it got hot and the humidity remained high. The air seemed thick, almost like you could cut it with a knife. It was even hard to breathe. After breakfast, we set out for the Kennedy Space Centre for a tour. This was an especially exciting day for us, one which we had planned from the beginning of the trip. So many major events had started here, everything from the first flight to circumnavigate the earth, to many different space probes as well as the Apollo Series that took man to the moon. The Kennedy Space Centre, which is operated by NASA, covers 110,000 acres on an Island off the Florida coast called Merritt Island. It is used for all 'manned' (or womaned) launches. Next door is Cape Canaveral, which is operated by the US Air Force. It is used for launching unmanned rockets, for instance, Global Positioning System satellites, communication (TV) satellites, weather satellites and spy satellites. NASA only uses a small portion of the 110,000 acres for their purposes. The majority of the property has been left in its natural state and is home to wildlife of many types. We initially intended to spend a couple of hours at Cape Kennedy and then return to our hotel and continue south, however once we were there we realized it would take all day to see most of the Space Centre so we decided to stay another day. The tour took us out to a large viewing platform from which we could see the two Launch Pads and the various complexes used by NASA for the Mercury, Apollo, Challenger and more recent space station programs. We missed the latest launch of the Challenger by only a couple of days and the shuttle was scheduled to return two days after our visit. We saw the third largest building in the world, which was used to house the Atlas rockets when the Apollo program was operational. We also got into the building where they were assembling various parts for the International Space Station, complete with a Canadarm (from home). The Visitors Centre has many relics from the various space programs, including early satellites, a variety of rockets and rocket engines. One of the more interesting programs they had was "Have Lunch with an Astronaut"; however we did not take advantage of it. This was one of the best tours we had during the entire trip. We were bussed between each building site and thoroughly enjoyed our day.

On the way back to our hotel, we were shown a bald eagle nest that weighed an estimated 500 lbs and was as big as a KING size bed. It is very old and the parents come home every fall, nest, hatch eaglet's then leave in the spring with their young and return alone in the fall. We passed it too fast on the tour bus to take a picture but it was certainly impressive.

Wednesday, June 20th. We decided not to stay today to watch the return of the space shuttle, which was a good decision in the end as it eventually landed in California due to the weather. Today was a riding day. We awoke to another scorcher with the temperature sitting around 88 at 8 am and rising. We tried our new cooling vests for the second time today with minimal success. They are Kevlar open weave vests with Mylar inserts, the Mylar inserts are soaked in water and are then frozen. Once frozen, they are inserted into the vest to cool the torso until the frozen materiel thaws out. They helped somewhat, however we did a long ride today so they didn't help in the latter part of the day. We left the Kennedy Space Centre area about 9.00 am and rode Highway A1A along the coast for a couple of hours, it was beautiful but slow going with lots of traffic on this 2 lane highway. We finally decided to switch over to Interstate 95 at Indialantic until we reached our first destination, Delray Beach, which is about 45 miles north of Miami. We had a great ride on I 95 and arrived in Delray about 4.30 pm, where we took our bikes to a Honda/Kawasaki dealer to arrange for servicing the following week, then dropped off a bunch of stuff at the timeshare we were going to stay at the following week.

We had a coke float to cool down before leaving Del Ray, this being the hottest part of the day, and decided to keep going south so we could ride on to Key West the next day. The weather forecast was for sun for only one more day before the weather that hit Texas moved into Florida. We had been so lucky lately, with bad weather in front of us and behind us; as we move on the good weather goes with us. Two days after we left the Kennedy Space Centre area, heavy clouds and rain moved in and the Space Shuttle landing was at first delayed and then diverted to California, yet while we were in the Kennedy Space Centre area, the weather was great and it was raining in Key West. As we rode south the good weather went with us all the way (God was smiling on us)! Anyway, we decided to push onto Florida City, which is just above the Keys, so we could get an early start the next morning. I think we had one of our best rides yet, as we took the Florida state Turnpike to Florida City and bypassed Miami. We rode about 300 miles that day.

Thursday, June 21st. We awoke to another beautiful morning, clear skies and rising thermometer. A perfect day to ride the causeway down to Key West, which is as far south as one can go in the southeast USA to mile "0", 129 miles south of Miami and 107 miles from Havana, Cuba. We got on the road about 7.30 am and headed south on US Hwy 1. We hit the Keys at about 8.00 am and had breakfast shortly thereafter at the famous town of Key Largo, home of the Humphrey Bogart film of the same name. After breakfast, we continued south along the Keys, across various islands and bridges (one bridge was 7 miles long) until we reached Key West, the most south eastern point of North America. When we arrived in Key West we rode down to the beach just so we could say we rode US 1 to its very end (or beginning, however you look at it). Riding the Keys is an interesting experience. The chain of islands are connected by a highway and bridges over the water. It's fun seeing nothing but water on both sides of the road for miles around. It gives one the feeling of riding on the water. We would be riding along one minute, enjoying the hot sun, the next a cloud came over us and dumped a solid wall of water; a short distance down the road it was dry and the sun was out once again. We have now travelled almost 8000 miles (12,500 kms) since leaving Victoria. The distance from Key West to our home in Victoria is 2789 miles **as the crow flies – assuming the crow is sober and flies in a very straight line.**

Once in Key West, we took a room for two days at the Courtyard

Marriot, unpacked our bikes and set off to explore the City. There was a free shuttle bus from our hotel to the center of town. Key West is a relatively small island with lots and lots of bars (Roney and I hardly drink, so we didn't help the local bar economy much). We did, however, shop, so I suppose that helps. We had a drink on the top of the highest bar on the island with the intent of watching the sun go down, but we were a little too early and left before that happened. We walked the waterfront promenade and watched buskers, then headed back to the hotel. The heat and humidity was just so tiring! After such a great day riding, it was time for sleep. One thing we did notice, Key West seemed like the capital of Lesbian and Gay lifestyle. It was hard not to blush some times!

Friday, June 22nd. We spent the entire day in Key West. Once again, it was hot and humid, even when the sun was behind the clouds. We spent an interesting morning downtown then returned to the hotel to check out jet skiing in the afternoon. The highlight of today was renting a jet ski for an hour in the afternoon. We took it out into the bay, which has very shallow water for several miles in each direction. After a minimal amount of instruction from the Jet Ski rental staff, we were off. Colin drove out of the bay and for about 15 minutes until he realized Roney didn't like riding behind, she wanted to try driving. Well, Roney only knows one speed on anything motorized and that is flat out. Within 5 minutes of her taking over, Colin went head over heels into the drink, yes, that's drink and Colin did - he opened his mouth to yell and instead inhaled water. Once Roney was sure Colin wasn't hurt and she was done laughing, he reboarded and off we went again. After a bit, she made another hard turn and, lo and behold, Colin went overboard again, only this time Roney came with Colin since he was holding onto her safety vest and kept hanging on when he went overboard. The safety shutoff worked well, the Jet Ski came to a stop and, after surfacing, we swam over and reboarded. We couldn't stop laughing while swimming back to the Jet Ski. We both went off once more when she cranked the ski around through a 180 degree turn and it dumped us again (that was three dunks for Colin). But she wasn't done yet. One more dunk and Colin was through. Luckily, the ski rental guy came out about that time and saved him from a further dunking.   We found the water to be like a very warm bath. The bottom was all sand and the water was not too salty. When we got back to the dock we were asked if we had fun and after telling them of our escapades the operator said he thought he had warned us there were reef sharks in the water where we had been riding ....great to get this information after the fact. We had a blast - Humm, maybe we need a jet ski - on second thought our waters at home are not as warm, we'll stay with the bikes! We ended the day with a lovely dinner at the Conch Republic Seafood Company and then repacked for our trip back through Miami to Delray Beach the following day.

Saturday, June 23rd. The sky was very cloudy when we started out and it was extremely humid, which it usually is before it rains! The traffic coming towards us going to the Keys for the weekend was bumper to bumper. We got pretty wet as we rode north, mostly perspiration mixed with a little rain. We arrived at Homestead, about 20 miles south of Miami, around noon and went to an Alligator Farm in the Everglades National Park. The Everglades are wetlands with various plants that grow in water and with a variety of creatures living therein, including Alligators and (SSSSSSSSS - I can't say the word). Anyway, Roney was very brave, she went in spite of the ever possible presence of SSSSSSSSSnakes.   Part of visiting the Alligator farm included a boat ride on one of those interesting looking airboats that are pushed along by an airplane propeller. The one we rode on was powered by a Cadillac 500 cubic inch V8 producing over 400 HP. It was impressive. The Driver was very good with Roney - he said he would try to make sure she didn't see any SSSSSSSnake's and he would take care of any that might happen along (none did). During the ride we saw a couple of good sized alligators. Their gripping power exceeds that of a full grown white shark. Part of the ride included several 180 degree power turns that had all the girls aboard screaming from the spray of the very dirty water and, of course, the guys saying nothing, just getting bug-eyed. The mosquitoes were really bad here and we were glad we sprayed down when we got off our bikes before we went on tour of the park.

We also visited the pens where they raise a variety of alligators - also interesting. And we didn't see any SSSSSS', even though they were having a SSSSSSS show when we arrived. After leaving the Alligator farm, we continued north on the Turnpike to Delray Beach and checked into our Time Share, which was right beside the Beach and which was very nice. The balance of the day was spent recovering from the heat by diving into the pool and getting settled in.

Entrance to NASA's Cape Kennedy facility, Florida

Roney viewing a launch pad at Cape Kennedy

Daytona Speedway, Daytona Beach, Florida

Taking a break along Highway 1A on Florida's Atlantic Coast

Mile "0", Key West, Florida

Everglades Airboat Ride Base near Florida City, Florida

Meeting a "resident", Everglades, Florida

CHAPTER 9 – DELRAY BEACH, THE BAHAMAS AND ORLANDO

Onward and upward is where we went, on this, week nine of our trip. This represented the half way point of our adventure. Both bikes continued to run well and we did not encounter any hurricanes, both of which were good news for us. The weather continued hot, with some periods of cloudy skies and occasional rain. We started this week out in Delray Beach, about 40 miles north of Miami.

Sunday, June 24th was a day off the bikes. Once again, it was a very hot and humid day. We spent as much time inside as we could, or in the pool. We did some grocery shopping and other housekeeping things (like laundry). After a dip in the pool we went down Highway A1A looking at some of the fabulous waterfront homes. Wow - In Delray Beach and in Boca Raton, the homes along the beach were all in the multimillion dollar bracket. Roney took lots of photos and we were totally impressed. We found out from the locals that the houses cannot be insured because of the hurricane threat. We saw lots of houses that had their boats docked at the back of their houses on the inlet. The hotels were huge and very impressive. Delray Beach really is quite a resort town and we enjoyed our stay there.

Monday, June 25 was errand day. We delivered both bikes to Delray Beach Honda for service. We have hit the 13,000 kms (8200 miles) since leaving Victoria. We had to buy a new luggage unit for the back of Roney's bike as the old one had literally shaken itself apart. Once again, it was time to ship more stuff home, as the bikes were, in a word, overloaded. We stuffed a large box full of things we no longer needed and shipped it home via the US Post. We also ordered new pipes for Colin's bike to cure his jealousy of Roney's pipes (he said it was so other motorists could hear him, even if they couldn't see him). We sought out the local library, finished and sent the previous week's newsletter and then picked up some needed supplies and packed for our side trip to the Bahamas (NO BIKES for the next three days). We bought a cheap flight out of Ft. Lauderdale to the Bahamas on Spirit Air for just over $40.00 each one way plus taxes. We reserved a room in the Atlantis Resort to check it out. It's the one shown in most ads and movie shots of the Bahamas – two very large buildings joined near the top with several walkways.

Tuesday, June 26. We got up early, the day was somewhat overcast but hot and humid and we were looking forward to visiting the Bahamas. We taxied to the local train station and took a commuter train to Fort Lauderdale Airport. Our flight left on time and 40 minutes later we were on the ground in Nassau. This flight is not much longer than Victoria to Vancouver and it was a steal at $300.00 round trip for 2 (including all fees). Try that between Victoria and Vancouver. We were taxied to the Atlantis Resort by a woman who was not only a taxi driver, but also a Minister. When we arrived we were dismayed to learn that we had booked into the 'older' part of the resort. The room was quite disappointing (you know the picture in the travel books does not look like the room when you arrive). Sometimes, it is a good idea to use a good travel agent. I thought I was getting us into the newer part of the resort, but not so. The room left something to be desired considering the price. It was, however, near a beautiful beach and we had a great view of the beach from the room. We were able to check in as soon we arrived and we spent the balance of the day on the beach, in the pools (of which there are many) and resting, eating and, well (you get the picture) relaxing. The Bahamas are a piece of paradise! Going there was a great idea, like taking a holiday from a holiday. In our shorts and golf shirts, we hardly looked the part of bikers; apart from the bowed legs and inability to open our hands!

Wednesday, June 27th We awoke to a perfect day in paradise (well named because the hotel is located on Paradise Island)! After breakfast, we spent some time on the beach and around the resort and then decided to head downtown. So off we went downtown and found the straw market. It was a bit disappointing as everything in it was 'made in China' (our new world reality). We spent several hours exploring downtown Nassau and liked what we saw. It has a very Caribbean feel and culture and the people are, for the most part, friendly. The beaches are fantastic, white sand and not just down to the water but out for quite a distance. The ocean was very warm while we were there. I won't say it was like taking a bath, but there was no shock at all going in. In fact, it was warmer than the swimming pools at the resort. We went to the Front Desk Manager and complained about the condition of our room (fingerprints on mirrors, stains on the shower curtain, mould, etc); things one should not expect in a 5 star resort. The manager agreed and gave us a discount, so complaining does help. We found out that there were other people complaining as well. One woman on the same floor as us referred to the rooms, with paint peeling off as "the ghetto of New York". There's not much more that can be said about this day, just sunning and swimming, what could be better.

Thursday, June 28th It rained overnight and it was raining steadily when we woke up. At one point we couldn't even see the hotel next door and the wind was blowing like hell. Roney said "maybe we're getting a hurricane". Well, an hour or so later, it cleared up a bit and the rain stopped, so still no hurricane. After Breakfast, we cleaned out our room and checked out. Upon checking our invoice, we found that the hotel had added the discount to our account rather than subtracting it, so back to the desk we went to get that straightened out. After checking out, we went looking for a taxi, which the hotel paid for to the airport. Well, the valet desk had quite a time finding a cab to take us at the hotel's expense. They finally got us one and the taxi driver told us he didn't like to take fares paid by the hotel, because the last time he did it took 3 months to get their fare paid (that says something about the management of the hotel). Here is what we thought of this resort, which, by the way, is well known. Atlantis is a very large resort. They have built parts of it and bought some existing buildings from other hoteliers. The building we stayed in was purchased about 5 years ago from Merv Griffin. They really push time share purchases; everywhere we went on the resort property, someone was trying to get us into a presentation to sell us a time share condo. We did not go as we had already attended one earlier on the trip. The grounds, pools, etc are awesome; there are waterslides galore, an aquarium, amazing displays of marine life throughout the hotel and many other interesting and fun things. But (and this is a big but) it appears that their focus is on selling timeshares and they are not putting money back into their existing property. Roney and I would definitely go back to the Bahamas, but we would not go back to Atlantis. The accommodation, for the money, was very disappointing. We had much nicer rooms for under $100.00 in the states. We went downtown and wandered around, checked out the market again and some of the downtown stores. We also went through a Pirate Museum that was kind of interesting. At the airport, our flight was delayed a couple of hours and then we had the train ride home. We did get entertained at the train station by a woman using her cell phone to give an ex-boyfriend a blast. We haven't heard the 'F' word so many times, ever! Finally arrived back at the resort in Delray around 11:30 p m, just after the skies opened up and rained cats and dogs getting us totally soaked going in to our room. But overall, we did have a good time in the Bahamas but we were happy to be back so we could continue our bike adventure.

Friday, June 29th The weather was okay today; back into the 90's with some clouds (you'd think we'd get used to it but, with the high humidity, we aren't). We went and picked up our bikes and, oh, were Colin's new pipes loud. He had no idea that the bike would be so loud with the new pipes, all he wanted was pipes the same loudness as Roney's but he was going to have trouble trying to sneak up on anyone in the future. After our evening ride, we picked up several items we needed and went back to the resort to pack. Went for a nice walk on the beach, along with a swim, which was very pleasant; the water temp was very doable here too. Had a nice dinner and returned to the resort and spent 3 hours packing.

Saturday June 30th   Got up early for what was to be another nice day destined to be in the nineties. We ate breakfast, checked out, finished loading up the bikes and set out for Orlando about 9.30 am. In spite of sending stuff home, the bikes were still really loaded. We no sooner got started out and Colin lost his glasses off the front of the bike while crossing an overpass and, despite several trips back and forth on foot over the overpass, they couldn't be found. That was one pair of glasses each that we had donated to the road gods. We travelled west from Palm Beach on Highway 80 through Runyon, around the bottom end of Obeechobee Lake and then north from Whidden Corner on Highway 27 through Palmdale, Venus, De Soto City and Haines City and on into Orlando. The ride was really hot, even with our ice vests on. The cooling packs tended to melt in about an hour, so, even with duplicate ice packs; we only got a couple of 'cool' hours. The ride was interesting. Central Florida is quite flat and mostly farmland. We travelled through miles of sugar cane fields, then, further north, we got into the citrus groves, but we couldn't see any fruit on the trees, although there were Georgians selling peaches along the roadside. We arrived in Orlando at; you guessed it, RUSH HOUR (they seem to have a rush hour here every day of the week!). We had a little bit of fun finding the hotel where we had a reservation, but once found, it sure didn't take us long to get into the pool. While in the pool, we met a nice young Hispanic guy who had had his bike repossessed. We gave him some advice and talked bikes as he'd seen ours' when we pulled in. One thing we have continued to find down here, there is a real brotherhood/sisterhood amongst motorcycle riders. Almost every biker waves to every other biker, including Harley riders. We have met many people who see us on our bikes and come over and, presto, we meet another interesting person. This was especially true at Service Stations throughout the States. We spent the balance of the day at our hotel and looked forward to being kids again for a couple of days.

Small bungalow, Delray Beach, Florida

Roney and friend, Disney World, Orlando, Florida

CHAPTER 10 – ORLANDO, FL TO NEW ORLEANS, LA

We spent most of this week in Orlando. Orlando has to be the entertainment capital of the USA, hands down. Disney World is huge, consisting of over 24,000 acres, far larger than the original Disneyland in California. For starters, it owns and operates a number of different hotels and resorts on its own property in various categories; everything from economy to luxury, there are more than twelve resorts owned by Disney Corp. Disney World is also divided into various theme parks; there's the "Magic Kingdom", which is similar to the California Disneyland, then there's Animal Kingdom, Downtown Disney/Paradise Island, Epcot Centre, Typhoon Water Park, another waterslide park and various other entertainment parks. In addition, there is a Sea World, similar to the one in San Diego, a Universal Studios park, like the one outside LA, Dollywood, etc. The list just goes on and on. It would take several months to see all Orlando has to offer. Of course, Daytona Beach, with its famous racetrack, is also nearby, as is Tampa Bay.

Sunday July 1st   We bought tickets to see the Dixie Stampede, which is a Dolly Parton dinner show at Dollywood. We had purchased a Disney World package while we were staying near the Kennedy Space Centre; it included 4 nights in a Disney resort, two 3 Day Park

Hopper passes (which allowed us to visit more than one park per day) and a meal plan. We would not recommend the meal plan as it was fairly expensive and the choices were limited. We arrived a day early (June 30th) for the package that we had booked, so we stayed in a hotel outside Orlando for one night and then headed to Disney World and checked in at our resort on July 1st. The trip was only 25 miles, so we only had to bear the heat for a short time. After registering, it was straight into the nearest swimming pool, another 95+ day with high humidity. The Floridians mostly stay inside during the afternoon in the summer due to the heat and humidity. That evening, we went by cab to the Dixie Stampede and had a great time. The show took place in a specially set up arena that allowed us to watch and eat at the same time. The horsemen and women (is that horsepersons?) staged a number of games based on horsemanship and silliness. They were divided into north and south, complete with north and south cheering groups in the crowd (we were on the side of the south). The dinner was good, the show was very entertaining and the "South" won.

Monday July 2nd We parked the bikes for the duration of our stay and took advantage of the Disney Transportation system (no parking hassles). All the parks were particularly busy, due to the upcoming July 4th holiday. We spent the day at Disney World and then went to one of the two Water parks, which had the coolest Wave Pool. It was massive and was full of people. The wave generator was quite unpredictable, but when it put out a wave it was awesome. It literally carried you along or pushed you over depending where you were in the pool. We spent the day playing with our inner children, a nice rest from the road.

Tuesday, July 3rd The Parks were packed, so the rides took time to get on, but we met lots of nice people in the lineups and generally enjoyed ourselves at Disney World. In the afternoon, we wandered around Downtown Disney and bought more souvenirs. These included a Mickey and Minnie Mouse, who were to accompany us throughout the rest of our trips as mascots on the top of the trunks on our motorcycles. Minnie became company aboard the Kawasaki and Mickey sat on the trunk of the Honda. Eventually, they rode all the way to Los Angeles from Orlando, quite a feat for two small mice. And Minnie turned out to be a real flirt – she would sit on the back of Roney's bike with her short skirt flapping in the wind, showing off her underpants to every passerby. We got plenty of attention from passing motorists thereafter, particularly from those cars with children. We tried the second Disney Water Park that afternoon to stay cool. The waterpark was definitely the place to be on such a clear and hot Florida day.

Wednesday, July 4th U.S. Independence Day was one of the highlights of our whole trip. We had debated earlier in the trip where we should spend it, as it's a big holiday everywhere. We were not disappointed with our choice of spending it at Disney World. There were huge crowds at the parks and most were wearing happy faces. One thing we really came to admire in the Americans is their outward show of patriotism. We both really enjoyed experiencing it firsthand and sometimes wish Canadians were as outwardly patriotic as the Americans are. It was very easy to get caught up in the euphoria of the moment. Everywhere the flags were flying, people sang their national anthem with gusto; they love patriotic songs, of which there are many. They are, generally, really great people and there is no doubt that America is a really great and powerful Country. There were many activities at the Park to celebrate July 4th, topped off by a spectacular fireworks display and special evening light show. Anyway, enough said about that. We thoroughly enjoyed our time in Orlando, but it was time to be moving on.

Thursday, July 5th The morning was overcast, but it remained humid (the humidity here is extreme after it rains and it had rained early in the morning). We got up, finished packing, checked out and hit the road. We had breakfast after we got underway and headed north on the Florida Turnpike, Highway 90. We passed through orange grove country and tried some of the juicing oranges (they are good). Pushed on north to Interstate 75, then west on Interstate 10, and decided to call it a day at 1.30 pm due to the heat and the fact that our cooling vests were anything but cool by this time. We checked into a hotel in a small city called Live Oak, FL just off Interstate 10 and put together another box to send home (the bikes just seem to keep attracting stuff and we just have to keep sending stuff home). After hitting the pool and cooling off, we mailed 2 boxes home, ate dinner and then went off to sleep. Tomorrow, we would be going through Tallahassee, the Capitol of Florida and site of the songs "**Ode to Billie Jo** (McAllister Jumped off the Tallahassee Bridge)" and my "Tallahassee Lassie". This was the point where I felt we would be entering the "real south". We had really enjoyed our time in Florida, but we were ready to move on.

Friday, July 6th   We awoke to another clear and hot day, another scorcher at over 100 degrees. We ate breakfast and hit the road at 8.30 am. We stayed on Interstate 10 to make the best time possible to New Orleans. We covered over 300 miles between 8.30 am and 4.00 pm and had one of our best rides yet. The words of that old rock song by Steppenwolf "Born to be Wild" that goes "riding down the highway, looking for adventure or whatever comes our way", came to mind. There's just something about ripping along with your very special someone, sharing the open road on motorcycles, roaring through the countryside with a new vista around every bend. We started out in Live Oak, Florida and ended the day at Gulf Coast, Alabama, having transited the Florida Panhandle. We passed through Tallahassee, the state Capitol of Florida and went around the northern edge of Elgin Air Force Base, the USAF's main armament testing grounds and passed the US Naval Air Station at Pensacola. We stopped twice for gas and once for lunch. Met more nice folks - the southerners are soooo friendly. Shortly after passing Pensacola, we crossed the state line into Alabama, then took state Highway 59 south to Gulf Shores, Alabama. The Alabama Gulf Coast is anything but what we thought it would be. It has numerous luxury high-rise condo buildings, resorts, some beautiful homes and it was BUSY! We checked into a Best Western on the beach and went in for a swim, which turned out to be the worst thing we could do despite the heat. After being in the water for only a few minutes, we both started to sting, guess what, the jellyfish were in and the hotel didn't bother to warn guests. So we got out of the water and we were both really sore and itchy! Roney had areas that felt like they were burning and they were red and swollen. So, we called the front desk and they said to use vinegar, which we didn't have, so Colin went and bought some and we applied it but it didn't really do anything but make us smell vinegary. So, we called the front desk again; this time they said use beer (I never knew that jellyfish didn't like beer!). We didn't have any and Roney decided there had to be something better. I left her burning in the room while I went to fetch dinner (shrimp and they were delicious) and found a remedy at a local store for jellyfish stings. I returned the hero, with dinner and beer and a cure for her burns (and the remedy did work) so **we** drank the beer. Spent the rest of the night OUT of the water, which was too bad, because the Gulf Coast seawater is as warm as we've been in anywhere and the beach sand is very fine. Fortunately, this was our only brush with jellyfish! An important lesson to learn though is to check the flags that are on the beach. It there is a black flag up stay out of the water. We did not see the flag but the front desk said it was out.

Saturday, July 7th Another hot one and reported to be the busiest traffic day of the year (many people take the week of July 4th off). So we saddled up and headed out into the busiest day of the year in the Gulf area. First, we tried a shortcut across Mobile Bay on a ferry (between Fort Morgan State Historic Park and Dauphin, Alabama), but it was so busy and we were not sure we could even get on that day, so we decided to go the land route, which meant doubling back the way we had come. A nice couple in a van that we met at the Ferry Terminal said they were going to do the same and to follow them. So we backtracked and then went north on Highway 59 to reconnect with Interstate 10. The Interstates are very fast, **most of the time**. Today, however, traffic was backed up from the George Wallace Tunnel (remember George, the state Governor for years) that goes under the Mobile River, near downtown Mobile, and it took us a couple of hours to go 10 miles. This was okay for people in air conditioned cars, however it was hot as hell on our motorcycles, which, when driven slow, produce heat of their own. Well, at least both our bikes were water-cooled so, even though we riders were overheating, the bikes weren't. Once through the Mobile tunnel, traffic picked up and we were headed west again at a decent speed, through the remainder of Alabama and into Mississippi, where we fueled up and picked up some tourist info. Then it was on through Biloxi and on into Louisiana and New Orleans. We covered approximately 200 miles; however it took us from 10.00 am until 5.00 pm, partly due to doubling back in the morning and partly due to the traffic tie up at Mobile. Once we were into New Orleans, Martha (our GPS) took us right to our timeshare in the heart of the famous French Quarter. It turned out to be very nice and in an absolutely perfect location, HOWEVER, we arrived on the afternoon of the third night of the second biggest annual event in New Orleans, Madi Gras of course, being the biggest. The "Essence Music Festival" is held in the Superdome each July and was being headlined by **Beyonce**. This was an especially important event this year as it had been moved to Houston in 2006 due to lingering problems from Hurricane Katrina, which occurred in 2005. The reason for it being extra special was that it was the first time holding it in New Orleans since Katrina, a sign that the city was attempting to get back to normalcy. Many streets were closed off by the NOPD (Police). It took us an hour to get our stuff into our suite and two hours to get our bikes to the parking garage which was only 4 blocks away! Every way we went was blocked by Police volunteers and we kept getting different directions to get to the garage from each manned roadblock we went to. Finally, a very nice NOPD officer sent us down a street to meet another officer, whom he radioed, and we got a Police Escort to the parking garage. Not only that, the Police Car escorting us had to back up because there was nowhere for him to turn around. That was quite an adventure. We finally got into our room with our stuff and our bikes put away at 8.00 pm. That was it, we hit the showers and then decided we had to go out and experience a little bit of the Big Easy before bedtime. We went out and inhaled some atmosphere and street life which we found to be fantastic and so energized. We can only imagine what it would be like at Madi Gras. Roney did so well today riding in the toughest conditions yet, heat and humidity, stop and go and go really fast on the Interstate. She's a great rider.

Beautiful Beach (but with jellyfish), Gulf Shores, Alabama

Action on Bourbon Street, French Quarter, New Orleans

CHAPTER 11 – NEW ORLEANS "THE BIG EASY" TO TUPELO, MS

Sunday - July 8th   Finally, some stationary time. We woke up to a beautiful day in "the Big Easy", hot and humid.   New Orleans was to be one of the highlights of our trip. We booked a couple of tours for later in the week and then went exploring on foot. New Orleans is a very different city than most North American Cities. It has a European feel to it and a strong French influence. Most of the street names in the downtown area are French and some of the buildings reflect the French influence, particularly in the French Quarter.   We wandered extensively in the French Quarter during this, our first full day in New Orleans. The French Quarter comprises an area of about 20 square blocks right in the heart of the city. It is most famous as the location of the annual Madi Gras each February. We especially liked wandering down Bourbon Street, the most famous street in the city. We wandered around the Decatur Street area and went to the French Market and the Flea Market (Roney's kind of place). We browsed for a couple of hours and then ate dinner in. This was mostly a recovery day, as we were still tired from the previous hot day's ride. Stop and start riding in 100 degree temperatures with high humidity is extremely challenging and draining. The previous day's ride had been a very trying one.

Monday, July 9th Another very warm morning, 88 deg by 8.30

am and very humid. We decided we would ride out into the Plantation Country and tour a couple of Plantation homes. We rode west on Interstate 10 until Colin thought we might run out of gas. This was unusual because we were generally very aware of when we last fueled up. West of New Orleans, Interstate 10 is elevated above the bayou and has no services for miles. When we neared the junction of 10 and 55, a sign indicated a town 5 miles down I 55. We turned off onto Interstate 55 and, five miles later, took the off ramp to a town that didn't seem to exist. Here we were in the middle of nowhere with low gas tanks. A man was sitting in his pickup truck under the freeway, keeping cool, so we rode over and asked him where the nearest gas station was. He was a very friendly rural Louisianan, wearing bib coveralls and with an interesting accent, he was just as we would have pictured a Louisianan to be. He asked where we were from and, when we told him, he said he'd never heard of British Columbia. He asked questions about our bikes and our travels, and then said he would escort us to the nearest gas station to make sure we got there without running out of gas. His name was Lou Pearson, he was 70 years old and he was as good as his word. At the gas station, we offered him some money for his gas and time and he said, "No, that's what neighbours are for". We visited with him for a bit, filled up and then headed south and crossed the "Mighty Mississippi" into plantation country. The plantations along the Mississippi were relatively narrow but quite deep. This way, each Plantation had access to the River to irrigate their land. At the time of the Civil War, there were hundreds of plantations along both sides of the river.

The first Plantation we visited was called Oak Alley Plantation, reputedly the most photographed Plantation of them all. A number of movies have been filmed here including "Primary Colours" and "Interview with a Vampire" (starring Tom Cruise). The front of this Greek Revival Antebellum Home (meaning BIG HOUSE) had eight large columns and two lines of 300 year old oak trees in two rows between the house and the Great River Road. These trees form a canopy between the house and the Road that is world famous. The tour of the home was done by a young woman in period dress. The interior of the home was very fascinating; life was truly good for those in the BIG HOUSE, except for the women, who had to wear those terrible whale bone corsets that sometimes made them faint. All that to get an 18" waist - what you girls did for men back then was crazy! The grounds were also something else as was the story of how the Plantation was built and its history. The home is on the National Register of Historic Places. We ate lunch, and then went to take photos of two 1920's original Ford cars and Roney made some new friends. Later we rode past a couple of other well preserved Plantations and onto the east side of the river, where we toured the "San Francisco Plantation". The San Francisco Plantation Antebellum home was quite different than that at Oak Alley. It was built between 1853 and 1856. One of the interesting surviving features of this Plantation was an original School House and Slave Quarters, which gave us an insight into what life was like for the less fortunate. Both Oak Alley and San Francisco Plantations host Weddings and other public events (what a place they would be for a wedding!). We returned to the City and went out for dinner on Bourbon Street, also known as Party Central USA. Bourbon Street is the heart of the French Quarter and is very much a part of Mardi Gras. The street really comes alive in the early evening when the Police put up portable barricades and vehicles are prohibited. This is done daily throughout the summer months. Open drinking is allowed on the streets, only glass and bottles are forbidden. Beer is cheap at $1.00 per plastic glass and every other type of liquor is also available. There are numerous Jazz Clubs, all putting out their own brand of live music, lots of Adult Toy Stores, peep shows and girls showing their wares in doorways, etc. For those of you who have visited the red light district in Amsterdam, this is about as close as it gets in the good old USA. It is highly entertaining just to walk up and down Bourbon Street and watch the goings on. After exploring Bourbon Street from end to end, it was time to enjoy dinner in one of the classier restaurants. We found one that served the best bread pudding soaked in a delightful bourbon sauce! The rest of the dinner was good too although, I don't remember what it was, but that dessert was unbelievable!

Tuesday, July 10   Another very warm and humid morning.

Roney went to a salon and had a manicure and pedicure, then it was off shopping for a sundress for Roney, which we did not find. After lunch we returned to our timeshare for a rest and then left for a bus tour of the city. This tour was fascinating. It was as much a tour about the aftermath of Hurricane Katrina as it was a tour of the City. The devastation wrought by Katrina on August 29, 2005 was extremely extensive. Here it was, 24 months after Katrina and one half of the population of New Orleans had not returned to the City. Eighty percent of the land area of the city was flooded for more than a month. Attempts were made to completely evacuate the city when it became apparent that Katrina was going to pass close by, but many people refused to leave. In the end, 1600 people died as a direct result of Katrina. Two days after Katrina had passed, levies collapsed due to high tides coupled with tidal surges resulting in flooding. Ward 9 was the hardest hit area. In some areas, flooding was a high as 12 feet. Government reaction in the aftermath of the storm was slow and FEMA, the Federal Emergency Measures Agency, the agency of the federal Government responsible for aid, did not act nearly as quickly as they should have. We were shown numerous abandoned neighborhoods, some of which may recover in the next 10 years and some that may never recover. In some areas, it was eerie to see empty shopping centres and neighborhoods, houses off their foundations, roofs gone, boats and cars wrecked. Much work has already been done to remove debris however it is estimated that it will take New Orleans another 10 years to recover. The people refuse to give up and it was clear that New Orleans would make a comeback. The spirit of the people is very strong as is their connection with their city. At the time we visited New Orleans, an estimated 100,000 New Orleans residents were still living in Houston, Texas. Due to the economic shock to many businesses in New Orleans, many of those relocated to Houston may never be able to return to New Orleans. Despite these challenges and the ever present possibility of a recurrence of such a calamity, the people of New Orleans are a resilient group and they will stay right where they are. You have to admire that kind of loyalty to their city.

The tour also took us to visit some of the old fashioned areas of the city that have beautiful homes and gardens. These areas were high enough that they did not suffer any damage from Katrina or the subsequent flooding after the levies broke. We drove by "Tara", the famous plantation home used in "Gone With The Wind". By this time, the driver was not stopping for us to take photos and several people on the bus were quite disappointed by this. Roney had had enough by this point; she said rather loudly "You can't just drive by Tara without stopping"! The driver was so surprised that he stopped the bus and backed up in front of Tara and let all the passengers off to take photos. He said that was the first time that anyone had ever expressed such concern at not getting a picture of the house. Leave it to Roney! Anyway, we got our photos and all the other women on the bus were very happy that she spoke up.

At the conclusion of the tour, we went back to the French Quarter to find Emeril Lagasse's restaurant named NOLA. We had no reservation and the restaurant was fully booked; it's always booked days ahead. After explaining that we were there all the way from Canada on motorcycles, the Matre'd said "Please wait a minute", returned a minute later and said "Follow me". He had set us up with a nice table for two and we had a fantastic dinner - WOW - KICK IT UP A KNOTCH - can those chefs ever cook. After, dinner, we went on to explore Bourbon Street again. We just couldn't get over all the action going on there and supposedly it goes on every day until dawn. They even bring in Louisiana State Troopers to augment the NOPD, to man the barricades. It's worth going to New Orleans just to experience the action on Bourbon Street.

Wednesday, July 11th Another hot, humid and beautiful morning. Today it was time for our Louisiana swamp tour. We were picked up at 10.30 am and, on the way to the swamp, viewed more of the devastated areas of the city as well as a NASA facility where external fuel tanks for the Challenger Space Vehicle are assembled. We arrived at the swamp and started our tour about noon. On the way to the Bayou, the song **"Born on the Bayou"** by Creedence Clearwater Revival came to mind along with John Fogerty's raspy voice. This was our best tour to date. We were taken out on a very slow moving river which is surrounded by swamp like areas (bayou) inhabited by many creatures, including alligators and snakes. Roney was extremely brave, knowing that snakes live in this area and 6 species are venomous (two of which are the cottonmouth and the water moccasin). She went with our guide's assurance that he would deal with any snakes we saw, including any that fell from trees into the boat. We went both ways on the river then up a tributary where we encountered Marshmallow eating alligators. The largest, named "Al", spent quite some time around the boat and our tour guide, Captain Nolan, a genuine Cajun, petted him for us (yes, we have lots of photos). He kept referring to the alligators as females and finally, one of our group bit and asked how he could tell they were females. His answer "they're soft, pretty and they smell nice". Well, we cracked up over that and he and the other boat captain got our two tour boats together and gave us lots to laugh about. On the serious side, they have a deep appreciation for the river, the swamp (Bayou) and its creatures, which they shared with us. They also showed us a very old Cypress Tree, called the Moonshine Tree, where moonshiners and swamp people used to congregate during prohibition to share moonshine recipes and try each other wares. Also, just two weeks before, Kelly Rippa of the Regis and Kelly Show, took the same tour with Captain Nolan that we took and talked about it on the show (being on the road, we missed it). We tipped the tour guide well for such a great day, especially for not seeing any snakes! At the conclusion of the tour, our bus driver told Roney that, on average, two snakes a month fall into the tour boats. I was so proud of Roney that, despite her enormous fear of snakes, she went on this tour and enjoyed it as much as anyone. We also found the location of the home of Brad Pitt and Angelina Jolie in the French Quarter from the bus driver. We walked by it later in the evening and took pictures. Brad Pitt has taken a great interest in helping the people of New Orleans recover from the devastation wrought by Katrina. On our return to the city we saw even more evidence of the damage caused by Katrina. As Hurricanes goes, Katrina was only a Category 3 when it passed by New Orleans (the strongest Hurricanes are Category 5), however the combination of a strong onshore tidal surge and high tides conspired to bring down the levies. Unfortunately, the Army Corp of Engineers have simply replaced the concrete levies that collapsed with identical levies; hence many people in New Orleans believe that they will suffer a similar fate in the future. Many homeowners were unable to collect insurance as the levy collapse was considered to be an "act of god", which are not covered. According to many people in New Orleans, the repairs done to the levies are insufficient and the chances of another collapse in the future are quite high.

Thursday, July 12   Another hot, humid day. This was the most challenging day to pack and go that we've had so far on the entire trip. It was hot when we went to get the bikes at 7.00 am and even hotter when be loaded them at 7.30 am but it did allow us to get away by 8.00 am. We would have left sooner, but our bikes were locked in a nearby garage until 7.00 am. We headed out for Baton Rouge, however, before leaving the city we tried to get onto the longest bridge in the world (the 24 mile Lake Pontchartrain causeway), but we just couldn't find the entry to it, so off we went to ride over the Swamp again on Interstate 10. Went through Baton Rouge where we turned north onto State Highway 61 to our destination at Natchez, Mississippi. Natchez is another Grand Old City of the south, smaller than Charleston and Savannah, but similar in architecture. Martha (GPS) took us directly to the Antebellum home called Monmouth Plantation where we had a room and dinner booked. Wow - what a house/mansion. It consisted of 22 acres, a number of out buildings, some used as guest cottages, and the main home. We had a beautiful room with a Queen size Four Poster bed that was right out of the 1800's, curtains and all. The entire home was restored in the late seventies, after falling into disrepair when abandoned in the 1950s by its previous owner. A developer from California bought it and gave it to his wife for as a Valentine's Day gift. The plantation is a work in progress and the grounds have been brought back to their former glory. The owners spend two weeks in California and two weeks at their plantation. The day was completed with a very special dinner in the dining room.

Friday, July 13   A hot morning in Natchez, Mississippi, ninety eight degrees at 10:00 a.m. and rising. We took a guided tour of the antebellum home we stayed in (which means big house built before the Civil War) after an incredible breakfast and then visited with various other guests and staff, answering questions about our trip and asking a few ourselves about the house. The house was absolutely chock a block full of genuine antiques. Everyone was so friendly it was hard to get away. We packed up the bikes and headed out for the Natchez Trace Parkway, which we remained on until we hit Alabama. The Parkway follows an 8000 year old trail established by Native Americans long ago and which was also used by early settlers and traders the 1600, 1700 and 1800's right up until the Civil War. It is very pretty, a fun and beautiful ride. The road itself is really smooth and relatively new. The trees on the sides of the road go completely across the road at times to make a wonderful cover from the sun. We could almost picture what it would have been like 150 years ago on horses. The "Trace", as it is known, stretches from Natchez diagonally across the Great State of Mississippi, then across the northwest corner of Alabama and north to Nashville, a total distance of 444 miles. It was deemed a very historic road and is administered by the National Park Service to be preserved in perpetuity for future generations. More than 100 different species of trees grow along the old Trace, making the scenery as beautiful and interesting as any road in North America and, best of all, the speed limit is only 50 mph and **it is enforced!** The Parkway goes through interesting rural Mississippi where we thoroughly enjoyed getting off the road for gas in the small Mississippi towns. This is what true motorcycle exploring is all about, and we didn't get stopped by a single Sheriff for speeding.

We rode 100 miles from Natchez north into Jackson, Mississippi, the Capitol, where we checked into another Antebellum home and found a computer to update our newsletter at a local market. Jackson has a checkered past as the Capitol of one of the most staunch of Southern States. It was the setting for the Johnny Cash/June Carter hit song "I'm Going to Jackson". The state flag still features the Confederate flag in the upper corner. We saw old homes with front porches overlooking the streets where people would hang out and visit with their neighbours and passerby. The state of Mississippi has come a long way over the past 5 decades; today the Mayor of Jackson is an African American. It was very evident to us during our travels in the United States that attitudes really have changed for the better.

Computers were not that accessible, but we tried our best to bring each day's events up to date whenever we got the opportunity. While we were inside, the sky had turned gray and black, the clouds were thick and the wind was howling; the sky was blue with the odd white cloud around when we went inside to use the computer! We knew we had literally minutes to get to our Inn and off load our bikes before the storm hit. We made it to the Inn in about 4 minutes and off loaded the bikes onto the sheltered porch and then moved the bikes to the parking lot. Immediately the rain just dumped on us as we were trying to back the bikes up and put them away for the night. Thunder and lightning along with torrential rain continued through the night and into the morning. The weather in this part of the country can change as quickly as it does at home.

Saturday, July 14   Today we started out with cloudy skies and a warning of flash floods from the weather service for the entire area. After having breakfast and loading the bikes, we left under cloudy skies, but thankfully with no rain. We got back onto the Natchez Trace Parkway and headed further into rural Mississippi. We stopped for lunch in an interesting small Mississippi town called Farmhaven. The only Restaurant had prices out of the fifties; Cheeseburgers for $2.00 (including fries) and grilled Cheese Sandwiches for $1.20. The waitress said the prices have been the same for the least 15 years - we even got a copy of the menu to prove it. The people were very friendly and very interested in our trip. They had the neatest accents. Not surprisingly, they had no idea where British Columbia was. By this point, we considered ourselves to be Canadian Ambassadors, educating southern souls about our Country. Shortly after heading north again, we passed through Kosciusko, which is where Oprah Winfrey was born and spent the first three years of her life. This town is just west of Philadelphia, Mississippi, which is where the movie "Mississippi Burning" was set. Basically, the movie was based on the true story of three Civil Rights Workers in 1964 (one African American, two white), who came to the area after a church used by blacks was burned. They were arrested and were later shot by members of the KKK with aide from the Sherriff's office. This brought much negative national attention on the small town, including an extensive investigation by the FBI. Eventually, 17 men were charged and received prison terms from 3 to 10 years in prison. These were pathetic sentences, considering they killed three young men in their prime, but it reflected a prevailing attitude at the time. Fortunately for all, those days are long behind us and more enlightened times are ahead.

The Trace has many very interesting Points of Interest along its length. A variety of small skirmishes and battles took place along the Trace during the Civil War and each of these is marked. We also came across a marker that indicated a number of Confederate Soldiers were buried in the woods nearby. Colin walked into the site and took photos of 13 headstones with Confederate flags engraved on them. All of them were marked as "unknown", however there were relatively fresh flowers on each, so it was obvious that someone was still caring for them. It was a very silent and solemn site.

We rode happily onto Tupelo, Mississippi, birthplace of Elvis Presley, where we stopped for the night. We checked into a hotel, unloaded the bikes and headed out (in shorts) to the Elvis Park. On the way, it decided to rain and hail on us, which hurt like hell, so we sought out an overpass to sit under until it quit. Then it was onto the Elvis Park, which was only 4 miles from our hotel. Elvis was born here on Saturday January 8th, 1935 at 4.35 AM (he also had a twin brother, who was stillborn). The 13 acre park contains the actual house that Elvis was born in as well as a museum and a gift shop. We toured the gift shop, then the museum and then went to the house, which consists of two rooms and is only about 350 square feet. Elvis slept in the same bed with his mother and father until they moved to Memphis, Tennessee when he was 13 years old. The people that work there love their jobs and know lots about Elvis. The lady we met in the gift shop met Elvis on his motorcycle in 1956 and talked to him for about 45 minutes and she's never forgotten it. The home was abandoned after the Presley family left. In 1957 Elvis purchased it after discovering it was for sale. He immediately donated it to the City of Tupelo, this being after he had hit it BIG. He bought it from the same man that had evicted his family years earlier when his father could no longer make the payments on a $180.00 loan he had obtained to build the home in the 1930s. Tupelo also has a self guided tour of various places in town where Elvis went to school and where he bought his first guitar. Above everything else, Elvis was an extremely generous individual with phenomenal talent. Everywhere we went Elvis is well thought of and admired for his kindness and generosity to others, often to people he just met.

Home damaged by Hurricane Katrina in 9th Ward, New Orleans

Beautiful Oak Alley Plantation, west of New Orleans

"Slave Quarters" home at San Francisco Plantation, west of New Orleans

Cpt. Nolan, Louisiana Bayou, west of New Orleans

Big "AL", 15 foot marshmallow eating alligator, Louisiana Bayou

Special seating for the suitor in Natchez's Monmouth Plantation – one seat for suitor, one seat for the "Belle" and one for mother.

The start of the beautiful Natchez Trace Parkway, Natchez, Mississippi

Civil War Grave along the Natchez-Trace Parkway

The Birthplace home of Elvis, Tupelo, Mississippi

CHAPTER 12 – TUPELO, MISSISSIPPI TO BRANSON, MISSOURI

In Florida we had to watch out for mosquitoes, love bugs, giggers, no-see-ums, cooties, snakes (which we did not see) acid rain and the remains of retread tires on the roads. The Natchez-Trace Parkway was clear of bugs, debris and retreads – It had to be the cleanest road we have ever ridden on!

Sunday, July 15th   We got up in Elvis's home town to overcast skies and the possibility of rain, but the temperature was still warm. We loaded the bikes, ate breakfast and hit the road late (10.30 am). There was no excuse for leaving late today, as we'd pretty much had the loading and unloading of our bikes down pat, we just slept in. By noon, it was sunny and 95 degrees. We rode the Trace out of Mississippi and into Alabama and then turned east onto State Highway 2, called the Lee Highway after General Robert E Lee.

We stopped for lunch at a cute little Alabama town called Tuscumbia, where we ate in an old fashioned Ice Cream and Soda Shop.   After lunch, we crossed Wilson Lake and continued on Highway 2 eastbound. Near Athens, Alabama, we passed within 15 miles of Giles County, Tennessee, where the Ku Klux Klan allegedly originated in early 1866, just months after the end of the Civil War. A native son, General Nathan Forrest, formerly of the Confederate

Army, was one of the first leaders of the KKK, which went onto infamy trying to suppress the newly emancipated African Americans. From there, we rode on into Huntsville, Alabama. Huntsville was the site of Alabama's most infamous event in the last Century. In 1931, a famous case occurred, referred to as the case of the Scottsboro Nine. Nine black youths were accused of rape by two white girls, all of whom were travelling by freight train towards Chattanooga, Tennessee. They were convicted by an all white male jury in what was to become one of the worst miscarriages of justice in the Deep South. The conviction was overturned by the US Supreme Court. They were retried and represented by an attorney from NYC, who attempted to have some African Americans included on the jury, but not a one was listed as eligible in the entire state by the state employee responsible for the jury list. They were tried again and convicted by a second all while male jury. Eventually, they were acquitted but not before being convicted several times and serving much time in prison, even after one of the girls repudiated her testimony and that of the other girl. As a result of this case, Alabama was forced to include African Americans as jurors, something unheard of before that case took place. It is disturbing to realize the tragic history of many African Americans, brought to the south against their will from Africa, forced to work for wealthy plantation owners and were still treated as less than human after the Civil War. Some degree of discrimination still exists, however America seems to be entering a much more enlightened age and full rights and participation of all of its citizens seems to be at hand. We should never again witness such sad situations as those that occurred at Huntsville, Alabama and Philadelphia, Mississippi.

At Huntsville, we took Highways 121, then 64 to Interstate 24, where we turned east and headed into Chattanooga, Tennessee. Just before reaching Chattanooga, we hit a thunder and lightning storm (with some hail) and had to hide under an overpass for half an hour. During that time, the temperature dropped to 61 degrees. We had covered about 210 miles in three states that day; Mississippi, Alabama and Tennessee. After leaving the overpass and just before reaching Chattanooga, we were speeding down the Interstate and a Tennessee

State Trooper pulled up beside Roney on her right side. She noticed his car and thought she was going to get a ticket for speeding. He dropped back as though he was going to pick up her license number, then he pulled up beside her again and, when she looked over at him, he smiled, put his thumb in the air and waved. I guess he just checked out the license plate, saw a great looking woman with her hair waving in the wind under her helmet, saw that she was from far off British Columbia and just waved a friendly "you go girl!" Roney then yelled over our two way radios "I AM WOMAN" !! This was the closest we came to being stopped by the Police anytime during the entire 29,000 kilometer (18,000 Mile) four month trip. All Southerners were friendly, including Police Officers. And, we never got nabbed in a single Sherriff's speed trap. We got to our hotel in Chattanooga and planed to ride DRAGON'S TAIL in eastern Tennessee for a second time the following day, this time without luggage.

Monday, July 16th   We awoke to a warm morning with a chance of rain. We headed out early with the intention of riding the infamous "Tail of the Dragon" Highway 129 a second time and to buy some more "Tail of the Dragon" souvenirs. We took Interstate 75 to Sweetwater where we hooked up with Highway 68, rode it to Highway 165, where we stopped for breakfast at a little 'mom and pop' gas bar & deli. The people there were really nice, with a typical Tennessee twang. Two local bikers were there at the time and we asked them for some advice about the local roads. One of them told us that 3 motorcyclists were killed WITHIN THE LAST WEEK ON THE TAIL OF THE DRAGON. They didn't know the details, however we later found out that two bikers died on a tryc when they hit a boat under tow on July 13th and another biker on a cruiser had died the day previous to that. We decided that, since we had already ridden the Dragon's Tail, we would just ride to the south end, buy some items and then loop back to Chattanooga without riding it a second time, and that's exactly what we did. When we reached the south end of the Dragon's Tail to buy our souvenirs, we had effectively completed a full circumnavigation of the Southeast United States (see the Route Map in the front of this book). At one point, we rode over a pass that was

5400 feet above Sea level. This surprised us as we had no idea that the Appellation Mountain range was that high. The days ride was very scenic. BC isn't the only area with beautiful mountain vistas. We got lucky too; rode all day without getting wet, although we saw rain clouds around us at various times of the day. By the time we got back to Chattanooga, we both felt that we had just experienced one of our best rides of the entire trip to date. And on top of that, not only were we circumnavigating the entire USA, we had now circumnavigated the southeastern United States (the former Confederated States of America) as well, including the Carolina's, Georgia, Florida, Alabama, Mississippi, Louisiana and Tennessee, missing only Arkansas and Texas (which we traveled through later). That in itself was a significant ride. Upon returning to our hotel, we met a nice couple from Texas who had trailered their bikes out to Chattanooga and were going to ride in and around Tennessee. There was so much rain in Texas with many roads washed out so, they came to Tennessee for their riding holiday. They rode two beautiful Harleys.

Tuesday, July17th was forecast to be a mixed bag of weather, but still pretty warm. We took Roney's bike into White's Cycle and Marine, the local Kawasaki dealer, for service. It was brought to our attention that Roney's bike needed a new set of tires, which we arranged to replace. We then set out to spend the day doing some local sightseeing. First, we took the Incline Railway to the top of Lookout Mountain, overlooking Chattanooga. A fierce Civil War battle took place here in 1863, with losses (killed, wounded and missing) totaling over 12,000. Even with such gruesome figures, this was a minor battle compared to many battles of the Civil War. Made us realize how horrible and large the US Civil War really was. The incline railway in Chattanooga is reputed to be the longest and the steepest in the world at 1mile and 1500 feet of vertical lift, however we have since ridden another one in Switzerland that is definitely longer. This one is probably the longest in America. On a clear day, 7 states can be seen from the upper viewpoint, although it wasn't clear enough the day we were up to see them all.

After going on the incline train, we went to a coffee shop at the base of the mountain that had the absolute best cinnamon buns you could ever imagine. We had to ask where they were made and to our surprise they were made just around the corner. Naturally we went to the bakery and complimented the baker and found out he was from California and we had a great chat about motorcycles and traveling.

Our next stop was an underground cavern called Ruby Falls. This proved to be a real adventure for Roney because she is claustrophobic. She did extremely well, going underground and, although she was nervous, she really enjoyed it. She took oodles of photos just to keep herself occupied and really enjoyed everything she saw. Ruby Falls is an underground waterfall roughly ½ mile inside Lookout Mountain and is 1100 feet below ground. To get there, we first took an elevator 260' down and then walked over 1/2 mile into the mountain. The cavern was full of stalagmites and stalactites of many amazing colours. At the end of the trek, we came into a very large cavern about 200' long, 260' high and 60' wide. A waterfall over 220' falls from the top of the cavern into a pool at the bottom. It was a beautiful site, especially so due to the coloured lighting used to illuminate the cavern. Would Roney go underground again, unlikely, but she was very brave this time (just like going on our two swamp tours in Florida and Louisiana, with the ever real possibility of seeing snakes). She's a brave and adventuresome one!! !

Wednesday, July 18th   A change in the weather back to hot. We were dragging our feet a little this morning so we didn't get packed and underway until after 10:00 am, just in time for the heat to really kick in. We headed out onto Interstate 40 for the ride from Chattanooga to Nashville, a distance of 130 miles, which we accomplished in just under 2 hours. That was good time considering the number of semis on this freeway, which has to be one of the busiest in the Nation. We checked into our hotel near Opryland on the north side of the City. Here we were in the heart and home of Country Music. On the recommendation of a good friend, we had booked a dinner cruise for this evening. We went to check out the Grand Old Opry and then went to a local shopping centre. We also took my bike into Howards Honda, as it was time to change tires on my bike. Both of us had now worn out a set of tires since the start of the trip (we had now gone 12,000 miles/18,000 kilometers). We spent the balance of the day checking out a large mall behind the hotel and then went for our cruise on the Cumberland River on the sternwheeler General Jackson. It started out as a nice evening on the River until the rudder failed and they had to return to the dock, where we ate dinner and watched the show while tied up. After it was over, they gave all of us a voucher for a future cruise (I think it's expired now!!). We wanted to check out the Grand Old Opry but we could not get parking anywhere near the building and there was a fairly high cost to just walk through and look around.

Thursday, July 19th   We were really back into hot weather. We got up at six, packed up the bikes, had breakfast and were on the road just after 8.00 am. This was definitely the way to travel, especially now that we would be headed into desert type areas further west and south.   We had a great run down Interstate 40 to Memphis and were checked into our hotel by 12.00 noon. Interstate 40 is an amazingly busy Interstate, as we've said before.   At times, we've encountered up to ten or twelve semis in a row. It gets very interesting when we tried to pass them and they were trying to pass each other.   Generally, the drivers are very good, however we've learned to be damn careful when going around them because, occasionally one wouldn't see us and would pull out into our lane just as we were getting ready to overtake. Also, between the ambient sound from our bikes, the wind, the semi's tires and exhausts we were unable to communicate using our radios. It was very challenging overtaking and passing semis and, in some cases, going between two rows of them in the middle westbound lane – lots of noise and semi's all around. But this is what keeps the Nation going. Riding Interstate 40 reminded us of the importance of truck transportation. After checking in to our Memphis digs, we went for lunch at an Elvis themed restaurant, then went straight to Graceland. We took the full package to see the works. Roney had been to Graceland before and knew what to expect, however Colin hadn't and was surprised that the actual home wasn't bigger than it is. The grounds are beautiful, consisting of over 13 groomed acres, with a horse paddock and numerous outbuildings. The house, however, did not seem big enough for the most successful recording artist of all time. Elvis, after all, defined our generation and was the King of Rock and Roll. He still generates more income than many current stars, even though he has been gone for years. Who will ever forget "Elvis the Pelvis"? We went through the house, which consists of a living room, dining room, music room, kitchen and his parent's bedroom on the first floor, all decorated in the early 70's style, which included shag carpets. In the basement, there is a large recreation room, a trophy room and a games room. The trophy room had some of Elvis's many awards and a lot of awards for his charitable work. Elvis was a very giving person; he gave much to many causes. The upstairs area is sealed off and not open to the public, so we didn't get to explore that area of the house. An outbuilding that used to be a squash court contained the bulk of Elvis's awards, Gold Records, Platinum Records, Grammys, etc. Awards filled both walls the very large room, which has a 16 Ft ceiling. We also viewed the graves of Elvis, his mother, father and grandmother, all of which are near the house. It also has a grave marker for his twin brother, who was stillborn. Across Elvis Presley Boulevard, we went through several museums, which are also part of the Graceland Development. One contains all the jumpsuits that he performed in (WOW), they were something else and it surprised us how skinny Elvis was. Another had his cars, motorcycles (yes, Elvis was a biker) and other toys. Another contained two airplanes, a passenger jet converted for luxury travel, called the Lisa Marie and a smaller Lear Jet. And right next door to Graceland, who'd have thought it. Right behind the museums is the Heartbreak Hotel, which has theme rooms and is part of the whole Graceland experience. You can stay in the hotel but we recommend you book well in advance. Elvis is definitely very important to Memphis's economy. He is loved and revered by everyone you talk to, both young and old. Interestingly, many of the visitors to Graceland that we saw were born **after** Elvis passed away.

Friday, July 20th   Another nice day in Memphis. Besides being famous as the site of Graceland, Memphis is also the place where Martin Luther King, the great Civil Rights Leader, was assassinated in 1968, after winning the Nobel Peace Prize in 1964 for his Civil Rights work. It seems that we find streets named after this great man in almost every City we have visited on this trip. The day was cloudy in the early morning but by mid-morning, the temperature was headed for the nineties. We went downtown for breakfast, found parking for the bikes and went to explore the Peabody Hotel. This hotel is reputed to be one of the most elegant hotels in the south east. It is definitely in the same league as our Empress Hotel, with a lobby that is absolutely opulent with marble everywhere and a lobby bar to die for. In the middle of the lobby is a large and beautiful fountain with five live ducks - yes ducks. The Peabody is the home of the original duck walk. Five ducks, a male and four females, spend each day between 11.00 am and 5.00 pm swimming in the lobby fountain. At 5.00 pm each evening, a red carpet is rolled out to one of the elevators, and to much fanfare, the ducks waddle across the lobby on the red carpet and are escorted up the elevator to their penthouse apartment on the roof. We watched the duck walk along with several hundred other people. This has to be the most effective marketing tool we've ever seen. What a way to pull in customers. Anyway, the story of how this tradition started is worth telling. Back in 1933, the manager of the hotel, a Mr. Frank Schuut and a friend went duck hunting in Arkansas. They apparently didn't get any ducks but they did get drunk on Jack Daniels and took two live decoy ducks back to the hotel. They couldn't take the ducks to their rooms for the night, so they put them in the fountain as a joke, and then went to bed. The next morning, they went down to the lobby and, lo and behold, there was a large crowd around the fountain thoroughly enjoying watching the ducks. Well, the manager decided to keep the ducks, and so today's idea of the duck walk evolved. Each morning the ducks are brought down in the elevator, they parade across the red carpet to the fountain, where they spend the day doing what ducks do, and then do the return route at 5.00 pm. The hotel has a full time uniformed duck master who oversees the daily event. After enjoying the duck walk, we went out and walked down Beale Street, which is considered to be the birthplace of the modern Blues and Rock and Roll. Many artists came to prominence here, such as

Elvis, BB King and many others. The Blues as a genre had its birth in the plantations of the south, but it came to popularity in Memphis, New Orleans and St. Louis. We completed the day by taking a tram around the downtown district. These tram cars were restored and look something like the cable cars in San Francisco. We did some late afternoon shopping and then returned to our hotel to prepare for the following days ride through Arkansas to Branson, Missouri.

Saturday, July 21st We got off to our best start yet. After a couple pieces of toast and coffee, we set out at 7.30 am on what turned out to be another hot day (the sun was smiling on us wherever we went now). We crossed the Mighty Mississippi into Arkansas and rode for a short while on Interstate 40, then turned northwest onto Interstate 55 to State Highway 63 to Walnut Ridge, then West on Highway 412 to Gassville, where we fueled up and had lunch. From there we headed west to Highway 65 and then north across the Missouri state line to Branson, Missouri, where we arrived about 2.00 pm. It was quite a long day's ride, but very scenic and very enjoyable. The roads were fantastic. Arkansas is agricultural in the eastern areas near Tennessee, along the Mississippi, and then it turned into rolling forested land further north. We stopped just over the state line in Missouri and booked several shows and then went on into Branson and found our timeshare, checked in and unloaded the bikes. It was a good feeling to have a week to just ride and explore the local area. For those who don't know Branson, it is a small city located in the Ozark Mountains in southern Missouri. It has developed into a mini Las Vegas, without the gambling but with lots of shows. For dinner, we went to a diner that featured singing servers. Each server has to audition to work at the Hard Times Diner and they are all excellent performers. A server will take your order and then sing a well known Country, Rock or Pop song and they aren't lip-syncing. It's a lot of fun and a great idea.

Later we attended an Eagles tribute show put on by an excellent band of 8 members, who sounded and acted just like the Eagles. We really enjoyed this show. We spent some time driving around Branson to get the feel of the place. The Ozarks are really hills, not mountains; however the Branson area is very hilly and challenging for riders. There is almost no flat area at all, you seem to be constantly on a steep hill and with unbelievable traffic you had to head out at least an hour before show time to make sure you arrived in time and to get parked. After a long day, we enjoyed just vegging out in the timeshare.

Entering Alabama from Mississippi on the Natchez Trace Parkway

Incline Railway, Chattanooga, Tennessee

New friends from Texas at our hotel, Chattanooga, Tennessee

Our favorite food store, Piggly Wiggly

Graceland Mansion, Memphis, Tennessee

Elvis's Grave, Graceland, Memphis, Tennessee

The "Duck master" at the Peabody Hotel, Memphis, Tennessee

The Ducks commence their daily "Duck walk" across the lobby of the Peabody Hotel

Chapter 13 – Branson, MO to Oklahoma City, OK

Sunday, July 22nd We just keep on enjoying great weather with more blue skies! There is no way that we could have experienced better weather throughout our trip. Our first few days of bad weather are long forgotten. Today, we decided to skip any and all shows and Roney went to the Spa at the Chateau. Branson has an absolutely stunning Chateau Hotel. It is set on a hilltop overlooking the local lake, the Ozarks and the City of Branson. The view is absolutely breath taking. Roney spent 4 hours being pampered in their spa while Colin ran errands. After a fairly quiet day, we went back to the Hard Luck Diner for dinner to enjoy the food and singing servers, and then toured some more of Branson on the bikes, which is so very enjoyable when they aren't fully loaded.

Monday, July 23rd Another clear and sunny day. Today, we decided to just veg. out. We did manage to do our laundry, read, watched TV until late afternoon and then went uptown to do a few things. In the evening, we went to an Elvis impersonator show that was absolutely great. This guy looked, acted and did a fantastic job of singing many of Elvis's best songs. After the show, we came back to the resort and finished last week's newsletter. It's really nice to stay in one place for awhile, as we covered almost 1400 miles in the nine days before we arrived here. That may not sound like a lot, but with the intense heat we've been experiencing, it does drain us.

Tuesday, July 24th   Another warm and clear day in Branson. Before our arrival in Branson, they'd been having a terrible summer with a lot of cloudy days and lots of rain. Here was another example of how we attracted and took good weather with us wherever we went. We're not bragging, really, we just attract good weather! We were good weather magnets. We spent the morning getting our bearings around Branson. It is a very hilly city, there is no such thing as 'on the level' here. We went to the old part of downtown, where we explored an old time 5 & Dime store, which was absolutely fantastic. A real "must see to believe". We browsed some other stores and then went for a two hour train ride to Arkansas and back on the Branson Scenic Railway. They have many very unique one-of-a-kind stores in old Branson that are fascinating to walk through. In the evening, we went to a variety show and dinner at the timeshare we were staying at and later went to an Old time Country Music Show that featured lots of old county songs (about lost loves and pickup trucks!!!). The last half hour of the show was a talent show for kids under 12 - 3 kids (2 girls and one boy) sang and were judged on their voices and stage presence. The boy won; he'll probably be a star someday.

Wednesday, July 25th   Another gorgeous day. We spent the day around our unit repacking and getting ready to ride out the next day. After packing, we went back to the beautiful Chateau on the Lake overlooking the city and did high tea, met the manager and found out that the Beach Boys were staying there (and we had tickets to their show). In the evening, we went to the Beach Boys concert where they sang all their great hits. The concert was sold out a good portion of the crowd were young kids, born long after the Beach Boy's music became popular and they loved it. It was like having their grandparents singing to them. For us, it was like turning back the clock to the sixties. We thoroughly enjoyed their performance. The crowd stood up and clapped and sang along with them. At one point, the lead singer got the crowd to pull out their cell phones, turn them on and then wave them back in forth in a blacked out room in time with the music and the look was something else. The band is still mostly comprised of original band members, with the exception of Dennis Wilson.

Thursday, July 26th   Just another beautiful day in paradise.   We dressed for another hot day of travel and were on the road at 8.00 am, heading south back into Arkansas on Highway 65. We fueled up at Harrison, Arkansas and then headed south on Highway 7. Lower Missouri and Northern Arkansas are home to the Ozark Mountains. Mostly heavily forested, interspersed with many lakes, the Ozarks are indeed beautiful. The countryside is quite rugged and contains a large valley known as the Grand Canyon of Arkansas. While not as deep and dramatic as the real Grand Canyon, it is nonetheless a remarkably beautiful sight. We continued south on Highway 7 to Russellville, where we fueled up again and had lunch.

After lunch, we continued south on Highway 7 into Hot Springs, which is set in a gorgeous valley.   President Bill Clinton was raised in Hot Springs, as was actor Alan Ladd (of Shane fame). Hot Springs is also the main centre for Hot Springs National Park. The City is quite old, with many heritage buildings and it is very charming. Roney had been here before and wanted Colin to experience the full Hot Springs Spa treatment first hand.   We checked into the Arlington Hotel, a hotel built in the late 1800s, to take advantage of the natural hot springs. We took a package that included a soak in their natural springs in a claw foot tub, followed by a sauna, a rubdown, then a lie down wrapped in extremely hot towels followed by a hot shower and exfoliation and last, but not least, a massage. It was great and an absolute must if you are ever in Hot Springs! ! It is an experience you will never have in your life anywhere else. Tomorrow we start heading west with 1 month to go until we have to be back in Victoria. We stopped in to visit one of the staff at the Wax Museum who Roney knew and had a nice visit.

Friday, July 27th   Another very hot and sunny day. We loaded up and left Hot Springs at 9.00 am and headed west on US Highway 270 to Needmore, where we fueled up and headed north on State Highway 71 to Fort Smith, then west on Interstate 40. The countryside between Hot Springs and Fort Smith, on the Oklahoma State Border, consists of gently rolling hills and heavily forested areas with several pretty little towns. We were both surprised at how nice Arkansas looked, it was totally different from the preconception that Colin had and was very different from when Roney was there last. I guess having Bill Clinton as a two term Governor and then a two term President can do wonders for a state.

We rolled into Oklahoma on Interstate 40 at about 1.00 pm, fueled up and then headed west for Oklahoma City. Eastern Oklahoma is fairly flat farming country, but is pretty in its own way. We fueled up once at Checotah, OK and continued on, arriving in Oklahoma City at about 3.00 pm, where we called a dealer to have the Honda serviced. They got us in right away, serviced the bike and treated us like royalty. We wish we could bring this Honda dealer back to Victoria so we could see him on a regular basis. While there, we decided to buy new helmets, as the ones we'd been wearing since we left Victoria were pretty much worn out. We also wanted to get gel pack covers for our seats as the old bums were getting pretty sore after anywhere from 6 to 8 hours in the saddle. The dealer didn't have any but they called around to other dealers and found two for us. After getting the bike ready to go again, we checked into a Hampton Inn, then tried to get a much needed good night's sleep but, due to kids jumping on beds above us, didn't succeed until around 2:00 am.

Saturday, July 28th This morning was a morning from hell, at least it was for Colin. The day started out really nice weather wise, but he had inadvertently turned Roney's handgrip heaters on the night before and that had drained her battery overnight and her bike wouldn't start. When the grips were installed, there was no visual indication that they were on - they had been wired directly to the battery terminals. We called a tow truck company and loaded the gear onto the Honda while we were waiting. The Tow truck driver arrived, jump started the bike, then left. After he was gone, we discovered that the front wheel hadn't been unlocked, which meant we had to turn the engine off to unlock the front wheel. We turned the bike off, unlocked the wheel, and, you guessed it; the bike wouldn't start because it hadn't run long enough to charge up the battery. We called the tow truck again, he returned and jump started it again and didn't charge us, he was a really nice Oklahoma guy. We reloaded Roney's bike and then it stalled, after the tow truck left of course, so we had to call him a third time. This time, when he returned, he gave us a jump start then spent a good half hour with us charging the battery from his tow truck. Once again, he didn't charge us anything extra, he even put his boss on the phone to talk to us about Canadian fishing trips, because his boss had been on one in Ontario and wanted to tell us how much he enjoyed Canada. We finally got under way just about 12.00 noon.

We wanted to take in the Oklahoma City Memorial, constructed to commemorate the people killed in the **Alfred P. Murrah Federal Building** that was blown up by a truck bomb on April 19th, 1995. We rode downtown and found Oklahoma City to be as beautiful and as clean as any downtown we'd seen thus far. A whole district of warehouses have been rehabilitated and turned into businesses of various types, the roads and sidewalks are done in bricks with fancy street lights, much nicer than downtown Victoria, called Bricktown. We went to the memorial, which was very moving. 168 Americans died in the blast including a number of children in the daycare centre that operated in the basement of the building. The blast, or blasts, were extremely powerful. A small portion of the destroyed building has been left as part of the memorial. The rest of the grounds have been turned into manicured lawns with 168 bronze chairs, one to represent each of the victims; also a wall of names of people in nearby buildings that survived. Next door is the museum portion of the memorial. The museum tour starts with a 5 minute presentation in a small room which consists of an audio recording of a meeting that was taking place across the street when the blast took place. Following this, visitors take a walk through an area depicting the aftermath with many photos of emergency workers and survivors. Timothy McVeigh was eventually executed for this unimaginable crime against his own Countrymen (men, women and children).

After touring the museum, we had lunch at what was one of the best restaurants we experienced to on this trip called Nonna's. The food equaled that which we ate at Emeril's Restaurant in New Orleans.

By the way, Oklahoma is one of the least expensive and friendliest states we've visited. It should have been a two day stop, however we didn't feel we had the time to stay longer on this trip. Amongst other things, Oklahoma City has been home to many famous people including, Mickey Mantle, Dr. Phil, Willie Stargell, Will Rogers, Brad Pitt, Reba McEntire, Ron Howard, Vince Gill, James Garner, Pretty Boy Floyd, John Denver, Dizzy Dean, Joan Crawford, Anita Bryant, William "Hop Along Cassidy" Boyd and Gene Autry.

We left Oklahoma City, probably the friendliest city we visited on the entire trip, and headed west on Interstate 40, for Texas. Just west of Oklahoma City, Interstate 40 parallels Historic Route 66. In fact, this day, we paralleled and rode on Route 66 for part of the day. Route 66 was called America's Highway before the Interstate Freeway System was constructed in the late 1950s and 1960s. Route 66 was the main route between Chicago and Los Angeles until the Interstate System came into being. We fueled up once in Texola, OK, then continued on in intense heat and were really relieved to arrive in Amarillo Texas, where they were hosting a Jehovah Witness Convention, so getting a room was challenging. We covered 260 miles in just less than 4 hours. We did get a room in a hotel that was hosting a huge family reunion, so getting to sleep was also challenging. Tomorrow, it's onto New Mexico.

Elvis impersonator, Branson, Missouri

Oklahoma City National Memorial, Oklahoma City, Oklahoma

CHAPTER 14 – AMARILLO, TX TO THE GRAND CANYON, AZ

Sunday, July 29th We awoke in Amarillo, TX, after very little sleep. The large family reunion was a loud one and it went on most of the night. Our room was adjacent to the bar (our first mistake); the hotel eventually had to call the police to quiet things down about 4.00 am. We really didn't want to complain as these folks had come from all over to get together, hadn't seen each other for a long time, so live and let live, we say. Today was another warm day, but we've moved from hot and humid to hot and dry, which is easier to handle. We saddled up the steel ponies and hit the road around 8.00 am, continuing west on Interstate 40. Just a few miles west of Amarillo is a very strange sight called Cadillac Ranch. We'd heard of this place before we arrived so we were on the lookout for it but only managed a quick glance at it as we passed by on the opposite side of the Interstate. Cadillac Ranch consists of 10 Cadillac's set in a field by the Interstate. Each vehicle has had its front end buried in the ground with the back end sticking out. Over the years, various passersby have stopped and painted graffiti on them and they have become a sort of folk art. Whatever the story is on how they came to be there, they are an interesting sight to see. Someone has a rather unique sense of humour or sense of art. And he must be pretty wealthy and eccentric as it seems he would rather bury his caddies after he's through with them than trade them in!

Old Route 66, or America's Highway, as it is affectionately known, parallels and, in some areas, has been obliterated by Interstate 40 in this area. When passing through Santa Rosa, NM, we stopped for gas at the Route 66 Auto Museum. This museum houses a large number of beautifully restored cars from the 40's, 50's, 60's and 70's. We spent a couple of hours looking them over and could have used even more time, but we had more sights to see elsewhere. Old Route 66 was about driving fun, sightseeing and uniting a Country, it wasn't about speed, which is what the Interstates that replaced Route 66 are all about. This highway has an almost cult like following. Route 66, also known as the **Mother Road, Will Rogers Highway** and the **Mainstreet of America** is the most famous road in America, bar none. It stretched 2448 Miles between Chicago and Los Angeles and was recently highlighted in the 2006 Pixar animated film "Cars". It was opened on November 11, 1926 and was used extensively during the 1930s dustbowl by people moving west. Route 66 was officially removed from the United States Highway System on June 27, 1985. Several States have since designated their portions of Route 66 as State Historic Byways.

As the song by Bobby Troup goes:

If you ever plan to motor west
Travel my way, the highway that's the best.
Get your kicks on Route 66!

The western part of the Texas panhandle was quite different from the east portion. It turned from prairie like to plains with sagebrush, then to wide valleys with flat topped hills. This same landscape continued into eastern New Mexico, where we turned onto Highway 84, and crossed over to Interstate 25, which we took into Santa Fe, the State Capitol. The setting of the famous capital of Santa Fe is arid, hilly but beautiful. We arrived in the middle of a downtown festival and all the major streets were closed. We checked for a hotel downtown; they were asking $350.00 a night and up for a standard room, so we decided to look outside the city. The city is boutiquish, very expensive and, we decided, not to our liking. We stayed in a Hampton Inn, just outside Santa Fe, for $159.00 plus tax. Two nights before we stayed in a Hampton Inn in exactly the same type of room in Oklahoma City for under $85.00 including tax! Our run today was 270 very enjoyable miles, so we were pretty tired and decided to stay in. Following Roney is hard work!

Monday, July 30th   There were a few scattered clouds overhead as we saddled up. We decided that a one night stay was sufficient in Santa Fe. If you ever visit Santa Fe, remember to bring lots of money! We fueled up and did a tour of the City. Almost every building in Santa Fe is adobe or imitation adobe; houses, town homes, condos, office buildings, government buildings, businesses of every sort. It's quite cool in that respect but it isn't a place we would go back to. We headed north on Highway 84, then west on Highway 502 and visited Bandolier National Monument. This is an old native cliff dwelling village used by Pueblo Indians several hundred years ago. After seeing Bandolier, we went on to Los Alamos. This was the site of the Manhattan Project, where the US developed the atomic bomb towards the end of World War 11. It was a very secret facility back then and has areas today that are still very high security. After passing through a guardhouse gate we drove around the area. We saw another fenced facility with a huge dish that is apparently used to listen to radio waves from space (UFO's anyone). This is a great area to use for secret facilities due to its remoteness.   After exploring Los Alamos, we headed west on Highway 501, then took Highway 4, then north onto Highway 126 to Cuba, NM.   About 20 miles up Highway 126, we came upon construction and the highway turned to gravel. After a slight mishap, we had to retreat to a small town west of Santa Fe on Interstate 25 called Bernalillo. The landscapes we saw today between here and Los Alamos were beautiful; high dry mountains, pine tree country with stark red cliffs and soil interspersed with desert like areas.

Tuesday, July 31st   We left Bernalillo about 8.30 am. The morning started out very nice and we had a great ride north on Hwy 550, with lots of curves and not much traffic, right through to Durango,

CO. The countryside was varied, from semi arid and rolling, where we started out in New Mexico, to gradually more mountainous and greener as we approached Colorado. By the time we reached Durango, we were at 7300 feet above sea level and the mountains around us were up to 13,000 feet high. We arrived without a reservation only to find that Durango is an extremely popular tourist destination, however we were lucky to get into a small room in a motor court, then we set off to explore the downtown area. Durango was founded in the mid-1800s; most of the buildings in the downtown area are from that era. There are virtually no new buildings in the downtown core which makes it really nice. It has the feel of a real Wild West city. Durango was originally established by the Denver and Rio Grande Railway. While downtown, we discovered the Durango and Silverton Narrow Gauge Railway, and booked an all day ride for Wednesday and retired early. This turned out to be one of the best surprises on the entire trip.

Wednesday August 1ˢᵗ We got up early and headed straight downtown for breakfast before taking our train ride. By now you should be able to tell that Colin is a train buff. Here's a little history on this line. Gold and silver were discovered in the 1880s in a town called Silverton, 46 miles north of Durango. Durango had rail service to the outside world but Silverton didn't. In one year, the 46 mile narrow gauge rail line was constructed into Silverton so that ore containing silver and gold could be brought out for processing. This line has remained in continuous service for 126 years since. Today, it only hauls passengers (tourists) and it is a phenomenal success. We took the 3 1/2 hour trip each way, with a two hour stopover at Silverton and enjoyed beautiful mountainous scenery, great weather and excellent company. We splurged and went in the Presidential car which had a rear balcony and that is pretty much where we spent the day. Silverton is like a preserved 1800s mining town with almost all of the original buildings intact, although only the saloon is still a saloon. The bordellos are now all boutiques. The train was pulled by a 1925 Baldwin steam engine that is exactly the same as the day it rolled out of the factory. It still burns coal, has a fireman who stokes the boiler by hand and it picks up water for the boiler; twice on the way up and once on the way down.

The train was sold out. This seems to me that something like this would work on the E & N Line on Vancouver Island. The building of this line in one year must have been a phenomenal achievement. Much of the line was constructed through canyons requiring much blasting and rock removal as it follows a deep canyon most of its length. We returned to our closet sized room, for which we paid $75.00 but at least the insects were free!

Thursday, August 2nd   We were up early, anxious to vacate our room and head out from Durango. We had the bikes loaded, had breakfast (Slim Fast) and were on the road by 8.00 am. It was overcast and we had to put three layers on to stay warm. This was a first in a long while. What a change in the weather. We headed west on Highway 160 right through to the FOUR CORNERS monument, where it is very flat. The Four Corners is the only point in the Continental United States where 4 state boundaries meet at the same point. A geological marker is set there with a cross to mark the point. When you stand on the marker, which we each did, you are in four states at the same time (Utah, Colorado, New Mexico and Arizona). The marker is on Navajo land and an admission is payable to them. It is also the border of the Ute and Navajo nations. We bought the usual T-shirts then headed southwest to go through the Navajo Monument Valley. This took us a couple of hours but, WOW; remember all the old Westerns with John Wayne, Alan Ladd, James Stewart, Jeff Chandler, Lee Marvin and others, where you see Red Buttes and other assorted rock formations surrounded by red desert? Well, this is where they were filmed. You can see many different figures in the various formations, including one that looks like it is giving the "finger". To say this was dramatic countryside is a real understatement. And what a great place to ride, long stretches of blacktop heading for far off horizons and beautiful scenery all around. Saw alot of other bikes today heading north, probably towards Sturgis, South Dakota for the annual bike rally. We rode Highway 160 to Teec Nos Pos, Arizona, and then took Highway 191 north. To top it all off, the weather was not too hot, not too cold, but just right. We arrived at our destination, Bluff, Utah, where we stayed in a nice lodge with views of buttes, mesas and desert.

Life just doesn't get any better. Roney continues to amaze Colin with her riding skills. The girl can really handle a motorcycle and look great while doing it!

Friday, August 3rd   Another hot day coming up. We were up early and had breakfast by 8:00 am in Bluff at the Twin Rocks Cafe. This cafe sits under a small mountain with two very tall rocks shaped somewhat like people. It's amazing that they don't fall off onto the restaurant. We hit the road for what turned out to be the one of most difficult day rides yet, at the same time the scenery we saw was second to none. The southern portion of Utah is absolutely amazing. We just can't come up with enough adjectives to adequately describe the countryside, but we will try. Utah has an incredible number of National Parks and a very varied landscape. As we headed north from Bluff on Highway 191 to Blanding, then turned west on Highway 95 we came to Natural Bridges National Monument. Here at the Visitors Centre, we learned that a National Monument is somewhat like a National Park, however a President can create a National Monument but not a National Park; only Congress can do that. Anyway, within the Monument, which is in a canyon area, are three very large natural bridges. Each one is relatively easy to view, however very difficult to get to. The largest is about 300 feet across and 50/60 feet above the ground. As with canyons, they are created over time by erosion. From there, we continued north on Hwy 95 through Glen Canyon National Park. This park is also very spectacular, with many unusual rock formations and very high cliff walls. From Glen Canyon, we carried on north on 95 to Hanksville, where we fueled up and then headed west on Highway 24, which took us through Reef Canyon National Park. Again, the scenery was breathtaking, even between the parks. At Torrey, UT we turned onto Highway 12, which took us through Grand Staircase Escalante National Monument, another beautiful site. During the early part of this ride, we reached an altitude of 9,600 feet above sea level and the temperature plummeted to around 45 degrees F and we rode in rain, wind, hail, thunder and lightning for a spell. From there, we went through Bryce Canyon National Park. This park is stunning. Its walls are carved so as to create the appearance of many people shaped rocks and the colours are varied from yellow through red and black. We'd never seen anything like it. After leaving Bryce Canyon, we went west to Hwy 89 and then south to Hwy 9 which took us through Zion National Park. We were awestruck when we saw Zion; it seemed that each canyon we saw was even more beautiful than the previous one and Zion was the best. The mountains in Zion are red and orange; some of them have vertical and horizontal lava lines. This Park must rate as one of the most scenic in America. We traveled 338 miles on this day, all of which were on 2 lane mountainous roads. We ended the day at a really nice mountain lodge named Majestic View Lodge with a wonderful mountain view in Springdale, Utah, just outside the Zion Park gate. This was the end of another amazing day; 12 hours in the saddle and sore bums.

Saturday, August 4th   We got up a bit later today, ate breakfast then headed out for the north Rim of the Grand Canyon. We had both seen the south Rim on previous visits to Arizona, but neither of us had viewed it from the North Rim. Very soon after leaving Springdale, we left the mountains and crossed into northern Arizona. They countryside was desert like and, was it hot, 98 degrees at 9:30 am. There was only one way to stay reasonably comfortable - go fast. So we drove the 65 miles of desert in record time. Driving in the desert was fun, the road was very straight; we'd reach the crest of a small hill and the road would stretch off for miles straight ahead. We eventually reached a forested area with a change in elevation and then drove another 50 miles to the North Rim, which is much less developed than the South Rim. A Native Heritage event was going on, so we watched for awhile and picked up a couple of trinkets. Then we walked out to a view point to see the Grand Canyon in all its glory. It is amazing from both vantage points and it was a perfect day to see it. It is truly breathtaking and it is easy to see why it is considered one of the seven wonders of the natural world. After spending a couple of hours there, we rode back to Springdale by a different route and, this time, spent almost two hours going through Zion National Park taking photos. Then we did a bit of shopping in town and went to an Elk Farm, where we petted the tame elk, then ate dinner and called it a day. We passed a small town just

10 minutes from where we were staying that had a flood just 2 days prior to our arrival. The water rose 5 feet and took the furniture out of many houses and floated an SUV a mile away. When it rains it rains and the water seems to stay on the surface. Roney continues to amaze me; she rides all day without complaint, better than most men, yet she rides fast and safe; she is always aware of what is happening around her and knows her bike inside out. Her hand strength has really increased, what with gripping the throttle, clutch and brake for hours each day. She is a very amazing woman and wonderful to travel with. The key to enjoying a long bike trip like this is to go with someone who enjoys the experience as much as you. We ended the day by packing up so we could move on into Nevada the next day.

Route 66 Auto Museum, Santa Rosa, New Mexico

Durango Silverton Narrow Gauge Railway, Durango, Colorado

Colin at Four Corners standing in Colorado, New Mexico, Arizona and Utah

Countryside near Los Alamos, New Mexico.

Unusual rock formation at Monument Valley, Arizona (kind of looks like we're getting the finger)

Roney riding Highway 160 in Monument Valley, Arizona (this was a very hot day!!!)

Twin Rocks and Twin Rocks Cafe, Bluff, Utah

View of Brice National Park, Utah

Colin riding into tunnel at Zion National Park, Utah

Roney petting "farmed" elk at Springdale, Utah

Hurricane Valley Heritage Park – to commemorate Mormon settlement, Utah

CHAPTER 15 – SPRINGDALE, UT TO SAN DIEGO, CA

Sunday, August 5th started out a clear and warm morning in Springdale, Utah, just outside Zion National Park. We packed up our bikes and started out about 9.00 am with the temperature in the low 90's. We headed west on Highway 9 through La Verkin and Hurricane, UT then picked up Interstate 15 for the trip into Las Vegas. By the time we got onto Interstate 15, the temperature was nearly 100 degrees, wickedly hot and dry, and increasing as we got through the hills in northwestern Arizona and into eastern Nevada. Then we dropped down into the desert and it really heated well up into triple digits and with a very nasty and gusting crosswind. By this time, we were sweating and frequently being blown sideways. Our cooling vests melted in short order and became a burden rather than providing relief. It became very hard to breath it was so hot. Several times, I saw Roney's bike leaning into the cross wind at an angle of at least 15 degrees and several times she was blown across a lane. It was impossible for either of us to remove our hands from the handlebars to even get a drink and we were dehydrating rapidly. There was no place to pull over, just straight freeway with traffic really hauling freight! We pulled into a small town called Logandale around 11.00am, filled up with fuel and water and asked how they could live in such heat. Their simple answer was, "stay inside in the air conditioning!" It was over 110 degrees F by this time. We drank as much as we could, then headed back onto the Interstate and arrived in Las Vegas 2 ½ hours later. This was definitely the hottest day we had riding on the entire trip. Martha took us to our timeshare, which was about 8 miles west of downtown Las Vegas, but still inside the city. We had never seen so much traffic there before and the new hotels were gigantic.

We couldn't get over how Vegas had grown since either of us was last there. We checked in, showered, dumped our stuff, had a swim in the pool, and then headed downtown on our bikes, like we just couldn't get enough riding in. We rode side by side up the strip, in bumper to bumper traffic, found a mall to park our bikes, since we couldn't find any parking lots that had any space. We had dinner then checked out Treasure Island, watched the ships battle, played a little on the slot machines and headed home, totally exhausted.

Monday, August 6th   After breakfast, we took Roney's bike to a local Kawasaki dealer and left it there for servicing and another new front tire, then we headed downtown to try and get some show tickets. We bought tickets for two shows on the same night, figuring we could drive between the two clubs between shows. The first was an Elvis Impressionist and the second was a combination Musical/Acrobatic show done in a hi-tech swimming pool in a specially constructed theatre. We did a little gambling, won some money on the slot machines then Roney went for a pedicure. The Kawasaki dealer couldn't get the right tire for Roney's bike so I had to phone around and then ride across the city to buy one at a motorcycle tire dealer, and bring it back to the Kawasaki dealer. Las Vegas is an interesting city to ride a bike in, but I made it, then picked Roney up and we returned to the timeshare. That evening we went back to the strip to the old area of Downtown. It's seen better days but they do have an incredible covered mall with an overhead video presentation about, you guessed it, America the Beautiful. We had a nice buffet dinner and Roney played on the 25 cent slots with $20.00 for 4 hours. Not a bad day!

Tuesday, August 7th   - Another triple digit clear day in Las Vegas. We went downtown and spent some time looking around then went to a boot store, where we met a very nice biker boot salesman. We bought new boots and got some local information. We then went downtown, looked around and later picked up Roney's bike. The balance of the day was spent in the pool and inside relaxing in the air-conditioning.

Wednesday, August 8th   Another hot one, but, hey, this is August in Vegas. We did some domestic stuff, like laundry and, that evening, we went to a jousting dinner/show that was really great. We bought a couple of water backpacks at a sports store to solve our problem of access to water while driving in strong cross winds without taking our hands off the handlebars. Just fill the backpack with water, wear it under our vests and attach the drinking hose as close as possible to our mouths and drink on demand! Wish we had these for the entire trip. At least we will have them for the next one.

Thursday, August 9th   - Another hot day. This was our last day in Vegas, so we decided to really explore the new part of the strip. We went downtown, parked our bikes and went exploring. First we went to the Luxor, the casino that looks like a pyramid. We had a buffet lunch and then went to play the slots and did pretty well on the 25 cent slots. Then it was off to the big casino next door where Roney hit first a $549.00 jackpot and then a jackpot over $200.00, the girl was hot! We spent the rest of the day going through various casinos and looking around downtown, then rode back to our timeshare and started packing for the following day.

Friday, August 10th   We were up early hoping to cover alot of ground before it got too hot. We decided to drive all the way from Las Vegas to San Diego, a distance of about 340 miles, which was a mistake. We set out about 7.30 am on a very clear morning and we missed a turn, wasting about 20 minutes before picking up Interstate 15. We made good time to San Bernardino, which we passed through about 11.00 am, where it was well over 100 degrees. About that time the traffic on the interstate was so busy traffic slowed and then slopped. We hit a total of 4 blockages on the way to San Diego and didn't arrive until 4.00 pm. We gassed up twice and spent some time in the gas stations just to cool off and rest our hands. Riding in bumper to bumper traffic in heat over 100 degrees is very trying. Roney is incredible for being able to do this and I felt very sorry for not insisting that we only go part way that day. For those of you who don't ride bikes, this may give you an idea of how trying it is during hot weather: You use your left hand for the clutch, your right hand for the front brake and throttle, your left foot to shift gears and hold the bike upright when stopped and the right leg for the rear brake. In addition, we had to use our left hand to transmit on our two way radios. When you get in a traffic jam, the left hand is constantly working the clutch (opening and closing to start and stop the bike) and after awhile it gets very sore; you can kick the bike into neutral once in awhile, but when the traffic keeps going and stopping, you have to go with the flow and it's easier to just leave the bike in gear. Roney was amazing; she handled her bike without any problem all day but had very sore hands by the end of the day. Needless to say, by the time we got to our hotel in downtown San Diego and got our stuff inside, we were more than beat. The only other riding day that came anywhere close to this one for draining us was on Interstate 10 from Tallahassee, FL to Gulf Shores, Alabama and from Springdale UT to Las Vegas, NV. As soon as we were checked in, it was off to dinner and then bedtime. <u>And here we were at another of the four Corners of the USA.</u>

Saturday, August 11th   Another hot day. We never intended to ride our bikes to Tijuana, so we left them at our hotel and took the tram service that was only 1 block away and goes to the border for $5.00 each. We crossed the border and got a cab into Tijuana and found it has improved since we were last there. Somehow, it looked cleaner than before. Tijuana now has over 3 million people. It even has a Costco and Wall Mart. A cab ride from the border to the well known main street was $5.00 (for both of us) if you take the yellow cab that says something like "economic" on it. The other cabs charge $20.00. Another hint is that you make sure you negotiate the cab fair and agree on the price <u>before</u> you get in the cab. That accomplished, we started on our downtown tour. The first item Roney decided to buy in a jewelers store was an eye opener for me, it was a series of 7 gold bracelets that were 14 k yellow gold that the guy wanted $700.00 for. Roney offered $15.00, the guy said "no, no, no" and put them away.

She went up a little and he came down a little then he said 'You're killing me'! On it went for over half an hour and she ended up buying all of them for $35.00 total. The guy thinks Roney's great because she bargains so well, he gives her a small present and then says she is 'ruining the Mexican economy'. Hugs were exchanged with lots of laughs and we were off to more stores and more demonstrations of her awesome bargaining skills. Another merchant told her she was a very fun shopper, then several others lined up to try and sell her stuff because bargaining is their way of life and anyone that can bargain that well is well liked. Let's just say, she cleaned up. We also bought the usual Tequila and Kailua. We had a most enjoyable day in Tijuana, before heading back to San Diego by tram. We cleaned up at our hotel then went out for dinner in a wonderful Italian restaurant recommended by an employee at the hotel. Then back to our room and packed up, ready to head to LA the following day early, to avoid some of the traffic. Yea right! ! As if traffic ever stops in and around LA.

Poster for Elvis concert (posted at Peggy Sue's Diner) in California
(tickets were $1.25)

Sign posted in Tijuana, Mexico store.

CHAPTER 16 – SAN DIEGO TO FORT BRAGG, CA

Sunday, August 12th   We left San Diego and were on Interstate 5 by 9.30 am. After 3 ½ months on the road, we were finally heading in the direction of home. Now, riding on the Interstates is always challenging, but more so in California, which is and always has been a "car culture". This makes California the most challenging state to ride a motorcycle in. Interstate 5 varies from 5 to 8 lanes in each direction and we had to stay away from the slow, off ramp lanes so that we could stay on Interstate 5 to our destination. That often meant sitting in a middle lane with cars on both sides racing along at their average speed, usually well over 80 mph and no Highway Patrol in sight. So it was a pretty fast trip to Anaheim.

There are more than 37 million people living in the state of California, which is 1 ¼ times the number of people living in **all** of Canada. More than 50% of California's population is non-Caucasian. California also has the 4th largest economy in **the world**, no wonder the Interstates, streets, roads and highways are busy. I guess that makes **Arnold** one of the most politically powerful men in the world. We checked into the Marriott Hotel near Disneyland and, boy, was it crazy. A large number of people were checking out, we couldn't get near the hotel entrance with our bags so we were sent to the parking garage. We asked a bellman for help once he had finished loading another vehicle and, with his help, we unloaded the bikes. We headed inside, the bellman took our bags to our room, got us a cab and we headed out for the Angles Stadium. This was our second ballgame during the trip. We arrived during the third Inning and got seats 1 row back from the visitor's dugout. Turned out to be a great game, the Angles won, of course. At the seventh inning stretch, we sang God Bless America and almost felt like Americans, after all by this time we'd been in the US of A for almost 4 months. We bought jerseys and caps, so we were official Angles fans now. We went back to the hotel and enjoyed a snack, then went to downtown Disney, which was a new section to us at Disneyland (no more large parking lot where you used to be able to park your vehicles). Disneyland now has three sections - The Magic Kingdom, Downtown Disney and the California Adventure. Downtown Disney is mainly restaurants and stores. We bought a Donald Duck, Goofy, Pluto, Pooh Bear and a Dumbo. The Mickey and Minnie that we bought in Orlando had now "officially" ridden across the entire US of A on the trunks of our bikes and could now be considered veteran bikers. Minnie flapped her skirt every mile of the way, we've no idea how many passersby saw her underpants, but we would rate the number very high. She was such a little hussy! But hey, we were noticed and no one hit us then claimed "oh you just came out of now where, we didn't even see you! We were visible and you could certainly hear us!

Monday, August 13ᵗʰ   Off we went to Disneyland for a full day of adventure and childish mindlessness. We went first to the California Adventure Park and we were one of only 300 people given a "Dream Fast Pass" that day. Our good fortune just never ended. We had used the fast tracks before in Disneyworld at Orlando, and they were great. For those of you who don't know what these passes are for, they allow you to avoid long lineups for rides and attractions and go in a short line with no time restraints. You present the pass at a ride and they give you a time to come back and, when you come back at that time, you get to go right on! These passes cannot be bought! You can't beg, borrow or steel them, they are a gift from the Dream employees that wander around giving out special items, so watch for these employees usually dressed in a very light blue outfit handing out something free. Without these Fast Passes we would not have seen half of what we were able to see that day. So we saw and did everything possible in both parks, we were very lucky to get these passes and would look for the person in blue who hands them out next time we go. We had a great day at the park, riding every worthwhile ride in the park at least once and just generally having fun.

Tuesday August 14ᵗʰ We packed up and left and it was H O T. We started out on Interstate 5 and went through the LA suburbs until we were north of the city and were able to get off Interstate 5 and get a room, boy we were both exhausted. We checked into a hotel in Santa Clarita by 1.00 pm where we stayed, slept and vegged out. Not a very long day but very hot and draining. The roads on this day were the worst we had ever been on because they were under construction. They had been milled and had those dreaded groves on them. This condition went on for miles and miles. We were to find out that the California authorities like the roads like this because it keeps the traffic within the speed limits and decreases accidents.

Wednesday, August 15ᵗʰ We had planned in the beginning to avoid using Interstate 5, which runs inland and where the temperature was predicted to get up to 105 deg. Instead, we took Highway 126 out to the coast and picked up the Pacific Coast Highway, Highway 101, which is far more scenic, curvy, more fun to ride and is cooler temperature wise. As we drove north along the Pacific on 101, it became much cooler; we even had to layer up! The ride was fun, lots of excellent views of the Pacific and lots of corners. At San Luis Obispo, we turned off Highway 101 onto Highway 1, the Coast Hugger. That night we stayed at On the Beach B & B in Cayucos, CA, a very popular beach resort area, just west of San Luis Obispo.

Thursday, August 16ᵗʰ We left from Cayucos and continued north on Highway 1, which is right on the coast. We rode through Big Sur, past San Simeon (Hearst Castle) and on into Carmel and Monterey (money towns). The Big Sur coast is wild, rugged and beautiful; often Highway 1 is well above the ocean. This was the kind of riding we lived for – up and down and round and round. It was windy and cooler as we arrived in Monterey. We tried to get into the famous Pebble Beach Golf and Country Club for a look around, but weren't allowed to do so because they don't allow motorcycles on the grounds. We found a hotel in Aptos, CA, near Santa Cruz for the night, and then spent an hour in the swimming pool.

Friday, August 17th We left the Santa Cruz area and rode Highway 1 back to Highway 101, then rode through San Francisco. Roney led and did her usually impeccable job, not one wrong turn, right onto the Golden Gate Bridge. We rode side by side in one lane across the big bridge and did a thumbs up. It was a beautiful day and the view, particularly from the bridge, was spectacular. Almost as soon as you cross over the bridge, there is a small road that brings you back to the coast. If you miss it you will miss a fantastic ride. We took the turnoff to Highway 1 at Marin City and, wow, this is one awesome motorcycle road. This is definitely the best motorcycle highway on the west coast for turns, twists, hills, hairpins, ups, downs, gearing up and down along with spectacular vistas. We passed through Point Reyes National Seashore with Roney leading the way and what a job she did. She was in her glory. We rode on and herein lies the next story. We were negotiating an inside corner; Roney accelerated out of it and Colin accelerated into the ditch. Roney didn't notice and kept on going and because of the turns, she didn't see Colin 'hit the weeds'. Colin's bike was stuck upright in the ditch and wasn't going anywhere. Three guys following in a car, jumped out to make sure he was okay; he was. Just the usual pride thing. Once again, the highway bar saved his leg. We got the luggage off, pushed the bike back onto the road and off Colin went. This probably took about 15 minutes. Luckily once again, there was no damage to the bike (Hondas are great bikes). Roney, in the meantime, was notified by a car that caught up to her, that her partner's bike was down. She was in an area where she couldn't turn around. So she parked her bike on the side of the road and started walking back. After a short distance walking uphill, she realized she needed a ride. She thumbed a ride with two surfers who were headed in the direction of the accident. In the meantime, Colin had reloaded his bike and started out to catch up with Roney. We passed going in opposite directions, Roney waved at Colin but he didn't see her in the strange vehicle. The surfers turned their truck around and followed Colin. In the meantime, Colin came upon Roney's bike and no Roney? Colin looked over the bank down at a beach when the surfers' red truck arrived and out jumped Roney. After making sure we were both okay, it was "end of story"! This was another example of our two way radios failing us. Anyway, everything was okay and we carried on to Fort Ross Lodge in Jenner, CA, where we spent the night overlooking the ocean.

Saturday, August 18th   Up and off to the north we went on Highway 1 hugging the coastline from Jenner. Once again, this was a fun day because of the curviness of the road and many hills. The ride was challenging, exhilarating and just plain fun. It is such a bonus when the road is crooked and scenic. We rode onto Fort Bragg, CA, where we spent the night at a beautiful B &B called Glass Beach Bed & Breakfast on the Mendocino Coast. There was a huge cloudbank out over the Pacific, lots of whitecaps and very windy. Again, we layered up, which was quite a change in the weather for us. Just one week left until our return home. We both had our separate thoughts about the end of this wonderful trip and all of our experiences and heading home to family and staying in one place for a while. Sort of happy, sad, thought provoking, wishing we had had more time in some places. We had a long talk that night about things we would have liked to have seen and didn't because of time constraints, because the time share weeks were booked ahead of time. Also the first part of our trip was too quick and we really needed another week to travel from home to New York State.

Roney rounding a corner on US Highway 1, Pacific Coast, California

Chapter 17 – Fort Bragg, CA to Victoria, BC Canada (The Ride Home)

Sunday, August 19th We started out from Fort Bragg under cloudy skies and 60 degree temperature, but, thankfully, no rain. This turned out to be one of the best riding days of the whole trip; 22 miles of curves, up hills, down valleys, along the beautiful Northern California shoreline and into the majestic Redwoods where Highway 1 (the Pacific Coast Highway) ends and we joined up with Highway 101. We made a couple of stops in the redwoods to enjoy the big trees and buy some souvenirs. The Redwoods are always an awesome sight; some of them are estimated to be more than 2200 years old. They are amongst the oldest living things on the planet; the species here are the *Sequoiadendron giganteum,* which grow only in Northern California and into Southern Oregon. Then we rode through to Eureka, where we spent the night and where we were able to find a computer to bring our Newsletter up to date! We ended the day by going to a buffet dinner, swimming in the pool and watching a good movie.

Monday, August 20th We left Eureka under partly cloudy skies and headed through Crescent City and into Oregon to traverse the awesome Oregon Pacific Coast. Along the way we passed through

Redwoods National Park, Prairie Creek Redwoods State Park and De Norte Coast Redwoods State Park. Everything they say about the Oregon coast is right; it is stunning with new beautiful vistas around every corner. Today we rode from 9.30 am through 4.00 pm, a distance of about 220 miles. While parts of Highway 101 are not within sight of the ocean, many parts of it were and the views were spectacular. By afternoon, the sun was reflecting off the ocean and displaying many colours. Coos Bay is nothing special to write home about; sort of a typical west coast resource town, but the surrounding countryside was much like our coastal home in Victoria, British Columbia, covered with evergreens. We spent the night there in Coos Bay and were feeling more like we were actually getting closer to home.

Tuesday, August 21st We left Coos Bay about 9.30 am and rode, with a couple of fuel stops, all the way to Seaside, Oregon, a place Roney and her sons Ian and Sean had stayed at a long time ago. The city had changed alot, but some of the arcades and attractions were still the same. We had a room with a view north up the beach, which runs for miles and miles. The beach is white sand and very wide, wider than Vancouver Island's Long Beach. There is a nice waterfront walkway that runs along the full front of the city, which we walked, then went to explore the downtown and had dinner. Horseback riding on the beach is a popular sport here. A long, but very enjoyable day but then, any day riding with Roney is enjoyable.

Wednesday, August 22nd This was kind of a melancholy day as we were down to only two more days of riding, and then our trip would be over. We awoke to overcast skies. Yikes, what's wrong here, we're supposed to be bringing sunny skies home! Anyway, off we went to reach Lynnwood, Washington, just north of Seattle. We stayed on Hwy 101, across the Columbia River, at Astoria, and then headed north towards Olympia and Seattle. We took Highway 12 at Aberdeen, went through Olympia, Washington's State Capitol and then north on Interstate 5 to Lynnwood. Just in time for rush hour, back into stop and go traffic, working our clutch hands for a good hour. Wow, do we have strong grips now after four months of using that clutch, gas and brake! We had a great ride over the 5 hours we rode today. We checked into a hotel in Lynnwood and went to bed early to get rested up for a last bit of USA shopping before returning home on Friday.

Thursday, August 23rd We spent our final full day before returning home shopping in the Seattle area. A fun day looking around Lynnwood, doing the usual Alderwood Mall thing, then Roney's personal favorite, the Ross Store, then Target, Fred Meyers, Sears, JC Penny, Marshalls and that pretty well wore us out. We packed for this last night on the road with mixed feelings, on one hand we were glad to be getting home, but on the other we knew we were going to miss the feel of being on the open road and discovering new things around every corner. Every day had been an adventure, nothing was cast in stone. The days had been pretty much ours to invent and experience as we saw fit. We were starting to talk about where we would like to ride next time and for how long.

After shopping in Seattle, we got to talking about the differences in prices throughout the US of A for everything from meals, accommodations, clothing and souvenirs and about customer service. There was no doubt in our minds that the Southeast (excluding Florida), is far ahead of the northern areas when it comes to customer service, friendliness and value for money. Reflecting on our trip, we realized how much we had come to enjoy the many people we met throughout our journey and the new friends we had made. America is truly a great, varied and beautiful Country. We Canadians are fortunate of have them for neighbors!

Friday, August 24th Well, finally it's arrived, the last day of our big motorcycle adventure. We left Lynnwood and headed up Interstate 5 with mixed feelings about ending such an adventurous trip. Just before reaching Mount Vernon, we hit patchy fog and overcast skies. We headed west to catch the Washington State Ferry at Anacortes, crossed to Sidney, BC and arrived home about 6.30 pm. We drove into the driveway and got off our bikes and looked around at the familiar gardens and house. It was good to be back .... tomorrow was time enough for reality to set in .... not now.

We phoned our kids to let them know we were back. It was nice to hear their excitement that we were home safe and sound. Tomorrow was another day, back to day to day living (its called reality). We were starting to plan our next possible motorcycle trip. We would like to ship our bikes to the United Kingdom and ride the entire UK, Scotland, Ireland, Wales and to the Isle of Man where Roney's relatives are from and where a couple of them still live. Can we possibly take in the famous motorcycle race while we are there???? Oh my, could this be our second book??

Well off to South Africa, to go on safari and visit Botswana, Zimbabwe, Zambia, Zululand, and Mauritius after a month rest. Not on bikes this time but you never know perhaps there is a chance we could do that another time .... Colin does like to travel! Maybe another book is there waiting to be written on our African safari adventure. We went on two safaris, one in Chobe National Park and one in Kruger National Park and have some outstanding pictures of elephants, lions, leopards, African wild dogs, Rhinos, Hippos, Wildebeest, Kudo, Impalas, crocodiles, Wild Boars and Dik Diks.

We hope you enjoyed reading our adventure holiday around the United States of America on motorcycles as much as we enjoyed doing and writing about it. We would love to hear from you. Our email address is roneys2007motorcycleadventure@shaw.ca.

Keep the shinny side up, ride safe and have fun!

At the Magnificent Redwoods in Northern California

End of the Line, home after 29,000 kilometers (18,000 miles).

Epilogue:

Writing this, our account of the best trip of our lives, has given us a chance to relive this great adventure. By the end of the trip we had visited 35 states (Washington, Idaho, Montana, Wyoming, South Dakota, Nebraska, Iowa, Illinois, Indiana, Ohio, Pennsylvania, New York, Maryland, Virginia, West Virginia, Kentucky, Tennessee, North and South Carolina, Georgia, Florida, Alabama, Mississippi, Louisiana, Arkansas, Missouri, Oklahoma, Texas, New Mexico, Colorado, Utah, Arizona, Nevada, California and Oregon). We enjoyed each and every one of them. We remembered the many great people we met along the way, Chuck in Nebraska who helped us with our bikes, the Capitol Police who got us into the US Capitol Building without day passes, Lou Pearson who escorted us to a gas station in Louisiana, the State Trooper in Tennessee who waved to Roney, the surfers on the California Coast that assisted Roney, the NOPD member who helped us to our parking garage in New Orleans, Capt Nolan in the Louisiana Bayou who made sure we didn't see any snakes, Mr. Toad for giving us a ride in his mint 1956 Thunderbird, and so many others. The people we met really made the trip very special for us. We will never forget the hospitality we received at all the various places we stayed. America is a great country not because of its military might, which is awesome; it is great because of its people and its landscape. We sensed that a great change was occurring in America during the course of our trip. Less than a year after we returned home, Senator Barack Obama, won the Democratic Party nod to run for the Presidency and it did not surprise us in the least when he was elected in November 2008. We viewed this as a very special event in American history, one that could only bode well for America. Virtually everyone we met during our trip was friendly and interested in our trip and, in many cases, envied us for just doing it. We certainly had some trepidation before we set off on this adventure, but after a few days on the road, they just disappeared and the trip became a highlight of our lives. If you have read this book and are contemplating an adventure, whatever it may be, I hope you will be encouraged to go ahead and do it – LIVE YOUR DREAM. You won't regret doing it BUT you will regret not doing it!

LESSONS LEARNED

For a confirmed biker, a trip around the United States is nirvana. There is no feeling of freedom equal to being aboard a bike with the wind in your face and endless roads to cruise. The variety of countryside and the scenery are awesome. There is an unexplainable feeling of adventure, which is impossible to equal through any other kind of travel.

Things that worked:

Preplanning is not a waste of time – the better prepared you are the more you will enjoy your trip.

Personal Business Cards are a great idea when meeting others.

A Realistic Budget is essential. We found it easy to keep a daily record of expenditures and on-line banking made access to money easy. We used a credit card for most transactions, which gave us a record of where we had been when we arrived home and assisted us with writing this book.

We recommend that you give yourself as much time as possible for your trip. We thought that 4 months was sufficient to explore the United States, but we agreed afterward that 6 months would have been better. As it was, we did not get into the New England states.

A Passport is the only form of identification to carry. By the time our book is published, everyone will require a passport to enter the United States. We have always found it advisable to make a photocopy of the photo page and store it separate from the Passport; in the event the passport is lost or misplaced you will have all the information you need to report the loss and have it replaced as quickly as possible.

Take a list of Important telephone numbers including family, doctor, health insurance numbers, bike insurance claim number, Warranty numbers (if under warranty) and keep a copy on both bikes.

A Basic Tool Kit for <u>each</u> Bike is also essential. You never know when a problem may develop and a basic tool kit can help you make simple repairs and adjustments.

Keep a second set of keys for your bike on your partner's bike. You will need them at some time on the trip!

Go over each bike each morning checking to ensure that lights work correctly, that nothing obvious is loose and that things are properly lubricated.

Service your bikes at regular intervals. We went through 2 sets of tires each during the trip. We kept records of the mileage of each service so that we would know when the next was due. Look after you bike and it will look after you.

A comprehensive Health Insurance Plan to cover health care costs is essential (for Canadians, $5,000,000.00 coverage is recommended).

Have a rough route plan with LOTS of flexibility. Keep someone at home advised of your general whereabouts at all times.

Heated vests were a godsend, particularly in the first quarter of the trip (Washington to New York). They kept our torsos warm, even while we were riding though a Montana blizzard.

When there is more than one bike, Communications are essential. The Chatterbox 2 Way units we used were good in urban areas and off the Interstates; however they were of little value on the Interstates due to ambient noise. Some form of hand signals should be agreed upon for use on the Interstates, as generally, the ambient noise was so loud we couldn't copy each other.

We had two Cell phones on a Telus North America Plan. This gave us

400 minutes of calling to anywhere in North America from anywhere in North America per month each. We used them for making reservations, setting up appointments for the bikes, etc. They were also available so that we could contact each other if we got separated and couldn't reach each other by radio. Voice mail is necessary for the latter to work!

Once we got used to using our GPS, it became a godsend in finding our way around. I would recommend having a GPS unit with an audio output so that you can hear, as well as see, the directions being given by the machine. Good paper maps are still essential as a backup and for daily/weekly planning.

Carry some cash and at least two credit cards, in the event one is lost, forgotten or stolen.

We also found an ATM card indispensable.

Buy a USA National Park Service Annual Park Pass. Ours paid for itself several times over.

Use UPS, FedEx or USPS to get rid of Souvenirs when they start to overload your bike(s). Also you will find that clothes that are no longer needed can be sent home such as heavy winter clothes.

For us, the use of Time Shares worked extremely well. It was nice to have a base to explore from and rest after long road trips.

A Newsletter or Blog (or keep a Journal) to keep friends and family up to date on your travels. We emailed a Newsletter to friends and family on a weekly basis. We found that libraries usually had computers that we could use. Our friends and family really enjoyed reading of our travels while we were away.

It is worthwhile to take something along to give away, i.e pins.

Digital Cameras are wonderful for travel. We took lots of photos and had plenty of memory cards. Just make sure you charge batteries when you stop for the night.

Always being prepared for the unexpected!

Keep An Open Mind: Whether you are a Civil War Buff, a backcountry explorer, love National Parks and Monuments, the Mountains, the Plains, Grand Canyon(s), awesome sunsets and sunrises, there is something on the road for every taste every day. We found the American people to be very friendly, helpful and full of wonder at two Canadians taking on such a trip. Without an exception, all were curious about not only our trip, but also where we were from. We became unofficial Canadian Ambassadors. We found all of the cities that we visited to be safe and enjoyable.

Carry a comprehensive First Aid Kit.

Pick one or two Hotel chains and use them. Most hotel chains give discounts, free nights or other incentives that can help reduce costs. We preferred either the Best Western Gold Crown Club Plan, Hampton Inns (Hilton HHonors Plan) or Holiday Inns Priority Club. There were also several places where we splurged like the Biltmore in North Carolina (can we afford to?/ can we afford not to?)

A Triple A or CAA Membership is strongly advised as many establishments give discounts to Members.

Take along some type of cover for the bikes – this will help keep the bike seats dry when they are not in use.

Pay special attention to your bike seat, you will happy you did. We used aftermarket seats (by Mustang) and added gel packs for additional padding. On top of that, we had pure sheepskin covers added as well. We still got sore bums after several hours, but at least the first few hours of every day were relatively pain free.

Water backpacks were invaluable. They allowed us to drink water and stay hydrated under any conditions, without removing our hands from the handlebars. We didn't discover them until we were most of the way through the trip, but after we did discover them we had no idea how we got along without them.

Things that didn't work:

Check to see if your bike has warranty coverage in the US (for Canadians). Our Kawasaki did not and we had a problem with a leaky fuel tank, which had to be replaced and we had to pay and then claim a refund from Kawasaki Canada when we got home.

Also, make sure that your bike's speedometer reads in Miles Per Hour for trips in the states.

References:

Bed & Breakfasts & Hotels:

Adams Inn, 1746 Lanier Pl NW, Washington, DC 20009 (202) 745-3600 www.adamsinn.com

Arlington Hotel, 239 Central Ave, Hot Springs, AR 71901 (800) 643-1502 www.arlingtonhotel.com

Brier Inn, 540 N Jefferson St, Lewisburg, WV 24901 http://www.brierinn.com/

Brafferton Inn, 44 York Street, Gettysburg, Pa 17325 (717) 337-3423 www.brafferton.com

Buffalo Rock Lodge, 24524 Playhouse Rd, Keystone, SD 57751 (605) 666-4781 www.buffalorock.net

Chateau on the Lake, 415 North State Highway 265, Branson, MO 65616 (888) 333-5253 www.chateauonthelake.com

East Bay Inn, 225 East Bay Street, Savannah, GA, 31401 (800) 500-1225 http://www.eastbayinn.com/

Fairview Inn, 734 Fairview Street, Jackson, MS 39202 (888) 948-1908 http://www.fairviewinn.com/

Fort Ross Lodge, 20705 Coast Hwy 1   Jenner, CA 95450   (707) 847-3333 http://www.fortrosslodge.com/

Glass Beach B & B, 726 North Main St, Fort Bragg, CA (707) 964-6774 http://www.glassbeachinn.com/

Goldsmiths Inn, 809 E Front St, Missoula, Mt 59802 (406) 728-1585 www. goldsmithsinn.com

Lambright Inn, 1501 Beck Ave., Cody, Wy 82414 (307) 527-5310 www.lambrightplace.com

Majestic View Lodge, 2400 Zion Park Blvd • Springdale, UT 84767 • 435.772.0665 http://www.majesticviewlodge.com/

Monmouth Plantation, 36 Melrose Ave, Natchez, MS 39120 (601) 442-5852 www.monmouthplantation.com

On the Beach B & B, 181 N. Ocean Ave, Cayucos CA, 93430 (877) 995-0800 http://www.californiaonthebeach.com/contact.php

Occidental Hotel, 10 N Main St, Buffalo, Wy 82834 (307) 684-0451 www.occidentalwyoming.com

Roosevelt Inn, 105 E Wallace Ave, Coeur D Alene, ID 83814 (208) 765-5200 www.theroosevletinn.com

Toad Hall Manor, 1 Green Lane, Butte, MT 59701 (406) 494-2625 www.toadhallmannor.com

West Yellowstone B & B, PO Box 1594, W Yellowstone, Mt 59758 (406) 646-7754 www.westyellowstonebandb.com

Helpful Motorcycle Dealerships:

Andre's Motorcycle Accessory Centre, 101-5701 17 Avenue SE, Calgary, AB T2A 0W3, Canada www.chrometoys.com (403) 248-0988 – Phil Boucher

Beasley Motorsports, 4317 Ogeechee Road, Savannah, Georgia 31405 (800) 959-3139 www.beasleycycle.com

Carter Powersports, 6275 S Decatur Blvd, Las Vegas, NV 89118 (702) 795-2000 www.carterpowersports.com

Climatech Safety Vests (cooling vests) http://www.climatechsafety.com/

Deal's Gap Motorcycle Resort, 17548 Tapoco Road, Tapoco, NC 28771

Howards Honda, 315 Donelson Pike, Nashville, TN 37214 (615) 883-3251 http://www.howardsmotorcycles.com/

Jim Anderson Complete Cycles, 4303 SE 15th Street, Oklahoma City, OK 73115

Matts Honda, 257 Mansion St, Coxsackie, NY 12051 (518) 731-8118 www.mattshonda.com

Motorsports of Del Ray, 1900 N Federal Hwy, Delray Beach, Florida (561) 997-6400 www.motorsportsdelray,com

Oklahoma Honda Suzuki, 3400 S. Sunnylane, Del City, OK 73115 (405) 672-1423 www.okhonda-suzuki.com

Waynesville Cycle Centre, 1899 Great Smokey Mnt Expressway, Waynesville, NC 28786 (828) 456-9710   www.waynesvillecycle.com

White's Cycle & Marine, 4917 Highway 58, Chattanooga, TN 37416 (423) 499-6000   www.whitescyclemarine.com

Points of Interest:

Appomattox Court House, Va http://www.nps.gov/apco/

Bandolier National Monument, NM http://www.nps.gov/band/index.htm

Beale Street, Memphis, TN http://www.bealestreet.com/home.html

Biltmore Estate, Ashville, NC http://www.biltmore.com/

Branson Scenic Railway, Branson, Mo http://www.bransontrain.com/

Bryce Canyon National Park, Ut http://www.nps.gov/brca/

Cadillac Ranch, Interstate 40, Amarillo, TX www.legendsofamerica.com/TX- CadillacRanch.html

Cody, Wyoming http://www.codychamber.org/

Colonial Williamsburg, Williamsburg, Va http://www.history.org/

Devils Tower National Monument, Wy http://www.nps.gov/deto/

Dixie Stampede, Orlando, Fl http://www.fortrosslodge.com/

Durango Silverton Railway, Durango, CO http://www.durangotrain.com/

Elvis Presley Birthplace, Tupelo, MS http://www.elvispresleybirthplace.com/

Everglades Alligator Farm, Florida City, FL http://www.everglades.com/index.htm

Ford's Theatre, Washington, DC http://www.fordstheatre.org/

Fort Sumter National Historic Site http://www.nps.gov/fosu/

Four Corners Monument www.navajonationparks.org

Gettysburg National Park, Pa http://www.nps.gov/gett/

Graceland, Memphis, TN http://www.elvis.com/

Gulf Shores, Alabama http://www.gulfshores.com/

Honey Island Adventures, Slidell, LA http://www.honeyislandswamp.com/

International Spy Museum, Washington, DC http://www.spymuseum.org/

Lookout Mountain Incline RR, Chattanooga, TN http://www.ridetheincline.com/

Los Alamos, NM http://www.visit.losalamos.com/

Kennedy Space Center, Florida www.nasa.gov/centers/kennedy/home/index.html

Mechanicsville Civil War Battlesite, Va www.mycivilwar.com/battles/620626.htm

Mile 0, US 1, Key West, Florida wikimapia.org/2096115/US-1-Mile-Marker-0

Mount Rushmore, Keystone, SD http://www.nps.gov/moru/

Mount Zion National Park, Ut http://www.nps.gov/zion/

Natchez Trace Parkway National Park, Ms, Al, Tn http://www.nps.gov/natr/

Natchez Tourism, Natchez, Ms http://www.natchezms.com/

Natural Bridges National Monument, Ut http://www.nps.gov/nabr/

Naval Base Cruises, Norfolk, VA http://www.navalbasecruises.com/

New Orleans French Quarter http://frenchquarter.com/

Oak Alley Plantation, Vacherie, La http://www.oakalleyplantation.com/

Oklahoma City National Memorial, OK City, OK www.oklahomacitynationalmemorial.org/

Orlando Tourism, Orlando, Fl http://www.orlandoinfo.com/

Outer Banks, North Carolina http://www.outerbanks.org/

Patriots Point, Charleston, South Carolina http://www.patriotspoint.org/

Peabody Hotel, Memphis, Tn http://www.peabodymemphis.com/

Route 66 Auto Museum, Santa Rosa, NM http://www.route66automuseum.com/

Route 66, The Mother Road, Information http://www.historic66.com/

Ruby Falls, Chattanooga, TN http://rubyfalls.com/

San Francisco Plantation, Louisiana http://www.sanfranciscoplantation.org/

September 11 Memorial, NYC www.national911memorial.org/site/PageServer?pagename=New_Home

St Augustine, Florida www.historicstaugustine.com/csq/history.html

Sturgis Bike Week, Sturgis, SD http://www.sturgisbikeweek.com/

Tail of the Dragon, Deals Gap, TN www.tailof thedragon.com

Trees of Mystery, Klamath, Ca http://www.treesofmystery.net/

US Capitol Building, Washington, DC http://www.nps.gov/nr/travel/wash/dc76.htm

Virginia City, Mt http://www.virginiacity.com/

Yellowstone National Park, Wy http://www.nps.gov/yell/

Wright Bros. Nat. Memorial, Kill Devil Hills, NC http://www.nps.gov/wrbr/

Zion National Park, UT http://www.nps.gov/zion/

Restaurants:

Conch Republic Seafood Company, Key West FL http://www.conchrepublicseafood.com/

Nola Restaurant, New Orleans, La http://www.emerils.com/restaurant/2/NOLA-Restaurant/

Nonna's Euro-Restaurant, Oklahoma City, OK www.nonnas.com

Peggy Sue's 50 Diner, Yermo, Ca http://www.peggysuesdiner.com/

Riverhouse Seafood, Savannah, Ga http://www.riverhouseseafood.com/

Silver Diner, Reston, Wa http://www.silverdiner.com/index.html

The Uptown Café, Butte, Mt http://www.uptowncafe.com/

Wyoming Steak & Chop House, Cody, Wy http://www.ribandchophouse.com/dre